LANGUAGE, DISCOURSE, SOCIETY
General Editors: Stephen Heath, Colin MacCabe and Denise Riley

Published titles

Stanley Aronowitz
THE CRISIS IN HISTORICAL MATERIALISM
SCIENCE AS POWER: Discourse and Ideology in Modern Society

Mikkel Borch-Jacobsen
THE FREUDIAN SUBJECT

Norman Bryson
VISION AND PAINTING: The Logic of the Gaze

Teresa de Lauretis
ALICE DOESN'T: Feminism, Semiotics and Cinema
FEMINIST STUDIES/CRITICAL STUDIES (editor)
TECHNOLOGIES OF GENDER: Essays on Theory, Film, and Fiction

Mary Ann Doane
THE DESIRE TO DESIRE: The Woman's Film of the 1940s

Alan Durant
CONDITIONS OF MUSIC

Jane Gallop
FEMINISM AND PSYCHOANALYSIS: The Daughter's Seduction

Peter Gidal
UNDERSTANDING BECKETT: A Study of Monologue and Gesture in the
Works of Samuel Beckett

Peter Goodrich
LEGAL DISCOURSE: Studies in Linguistics, Rhetoric and Legal Analysis

Piers Gray
MARGINAL MEN: Edward Thomas, Ivor Gurney, J. R. Ackerley

Paul Hirst
ON LAW AND IDEOLOGY

Ian Hunter
CULTURE AND GOVERNMENT: The Emergence of Literary Education

Andreas Huyssen
AFTER THE GREAT DIVIDE: Modernism, Mass Culture
and Postmodernism

Nigel Leask
THE POLITICS OF IMAGINATION
IN COLERIDGE'S CRITICAL THOUGHT

Michael Lynn-George
EPOS: WORD, NARRATIVE AND THE ILIAD

W0192934

Colin MacCabe
JAMES JOYCE AND THE REVOLUTION OF THE WORD
THE TALKING CURE: Essays on Psychoanalysis and Language (editor)

Louis Marin
PORTRAIT OF THE KING

Christian Metz
PSYCHOANALYSIS AND CINEMA: The Imaginary Signifier

Jean-Claude Milner
FOR THE LOVE OF LANGUAGE

Jeffrey Minson
GENEALOGIES OF MORALS: Nietzsche, Foucault, Donzelot and the
Eccentricity of Ethics

Laura Mulvey
VISUAL AND OTHER PLEASURES

Douglas Oliver
POETRY AND NARRATIVE IN PERFORMANCE

Michel Pêcheux
LANGUAGE, SEMANTICS AND IDEOLOGY

Jean-Michel Rabaté
LANGUAGE, SEXUALITY AND IDEOLOGY IN EZRA POUND'S *CANTOS*

Denise Riley
'AM I THAT NAME?': Feminism and the Category of 'Women' in History

Jacqueline Rose
THE CASE OF PETER PAN
or THE IMPOSSIBILITY OF CHILDREN'S FICTION

Brian Rotman
SIGNIFYING NOTHING: The Semiotics of Zero

Michael Ryan
POLITICS AND CULTURE: Working Hypotheses
for a Post-Revolutionary Society

Raymond Tallis
NOT SAUSSURE: A Critique of Post-Saussurean Literary Theory

David Trotter
CIRCULATION: Defoe, Dickens and the Economies of the Novel
THE MAKING OF THE READER: Language and Subjectivity in Modern
American, English and Irish Poetry

Cornel West
THE AMERICAN EVASION OF PHILOSOPHY

Peter Womack
IMPROVEMENT AND ROMANCE:
Constructing the Myth of the Highlands

Marginal Men

Edward Thomas; Ivor Gurney; J. R. Ackerley

PIERS GRAY

Department of English
University of Hong Kong

MACMILLAN

First published 1991

Published by
MACMILLAN ACADEMIC AND PROFESSIONAL LTD
Houndmills, Basingstoke, Hampshire RG21 2XS
and London

Companies and representatives
throughout the world

British Library Cataloguing in Publication Data
Gray, Piers
Marginal Men: Edward Thomas; Ivor Gurney; J. R. Ackerley
 – (Language, discourse, society series)
1. English Literature 1900 –   – Biographies   – Collections
I. Title   II. Series
820.9′00912
ISBN 978-1-349-08139-4   ISBN 978-1-349-08137-0 (eBook)
DOI 10.1007/978-1-349-08137-0

Series Standing Order

If you would like to receive future titles in this series as they are
published, you can make use of our standing order facility. To
place a standing order please contact your bookseller or, in case
of difficulty, write to us at the address below with your name
and address and the name of the series. Please state with which
title you wish to begin your standing order. (If you live outside
the United Kingdom we may not have the rights in your area, in
which case we will forward your order to the publisher concerned.)

Customer Services Department, Macmillan Distribution Ltd.
Houndmills, Basingstoke, Hampshire, RG21 2XS, England.

For Simon and Beryl

. . . the mind is the most terrible force in the world principally in this, that it is the only force that can defend us against itself.

Wallace Stevens (*Adagia*)

One of the unhappy necessities of human existence is that we have to 'find things out for ourselves'.

T. S. Eliot ('Baudelaire')

Contents

Acknowledgements

Quotations from the published works of J. R. Ackerley are by permission of Francis King and the Ackerley Estate.

Grateful acknowledgement is made to P. J. Kavanagh for kind permission to quote from his Introduction to *Collected Poems of Ivor Gurney*; and further, P. J. Kavanagh and Oxford University Press for permission to quote from *Collected Poems of Ivor Gurney*.

Grateful acknowledgement is made to L. F. Haber for kind permission to quote from *The Poisonous Cloud*, Oxford University Press.

Philip Larkin, 'MCMXIV' is reprinted by permission of Faber & Faber Ltd., from *The Whitsun Weddings* by Philip Larkin.

Helen Thomas, 'Ivor Gurney' is reprinted by permission of Carcanet Press from *Time and Again* (reprinted in *Under Storm's Wing*, Carcanet Press Ltd.) by Helen Thomas.

Chapter 1, *The Childhood of Edward Thomas*, originally appeared in *Critical Quarterly*, published by Manchester University Press. It was reprinted, with corrections, in *Futures for English*, edited by Colin MacCabe, Manchester University Press. Grateful acknowledgement is made for permission to republish this piece.

I would like to thank the following colleagues at the University of Hong Kong for their valuable comments and criticisms at different stages of this book's progress: Mimi Chan, Murray Groves, Helen Kwok, Jack Lowcock and John Preston; furthermore, I owe much to Jeff Henderson, Douglas Kerr and James Lethbridge for being so generous with information and advice.

I am extremely grateful to Jeremy Prynne and Frank Kermode for the wisdom of their conversation and to Jeremy Prynne in particular for his comments and suggestions about structure and tone.

Colin MacCabe encouraged and supported the development of the piece from the beginning. Samantha Chan typed and retyped the manuscript; I am grateful to her and to Sally Stewart who read and corrected the proofs – any mistakes which remain are mine.

Finally – to Annie my gratitude for the gift of present laughter.

Introduction:
Inventing Traditions

Il est plus aisé de connaître l'homme en général que de connaître un homme en particulier.[1]

I

A corollary to this maxim might be: feeling the life of a single other existence or making felt, to another, one's own single existence is a virtue unique to imaginative writing. '"Life"' – as F. R. Leavis observes of Montale's *Xenia* – 'is a necessary word, but "life" is concretely "there" only in individual lives'.[2] What follows hereafter is a version of the attempt to understand 'life' through the written lives of three men: three writers whose imaginations struggled to express their own and others' particularities. Understanding their words provokes a belief in the ideal of understanding their lives: understanding their lives justifies the attempt to understand their words – to do criticism. And this is simply the confirmation of the extraordinary illusion of language – somehow arbitrary sounds and signs are naturalized and the isolation of selves is transcended.

II

That, of course, is a paradoxical justification of the writer's egocentricity. Only by engaging with the self to a sufficiently obsessive degree can the act of writing about the self begin and its solitude thus be transformed. To that extent, the 'writing self' is its own authority, answerable to no one. Making over language, it fantasizes in the defeat of solitude; or, in failure consoles itself that solitude at least is the necessary precondition of the need to articulate: 'And weep the more because I weep in vain'.[3]

1

III

The creation of a voice, or voices, true to the conception of individuated, particularized, selves (and presumably the self may further have many selves) is the act of an author. And it is an authentic act in as much as we recognize the distinctness, the apartness of that voice. Paradoxically, then, the act of communication is equally an act of isolation, of particularization. The degree of successful isolation measures the extent to which we can deem the author to be sincere. Sincerity is a function then of realising distinct 'lives'. To that extent it has nothing to do with 'truthfulness' – who is more sincere than the man who confesses that he tells lies?

I Travestimenti

. . .
Risulta così sempre vana
l'arte dello sdoppiamento:
abbiamo voluto camuffarci
come i prostituti nottivaghi
per nascondere meglio le nostre piaghe
ma è inutile, basta guardarci.

Disguises

. . .
Thus the art of the split personality
always turns out to be useless.
We wanted to camouflage ourselves
like the transvestites wandering by night
the better to hide our wounds,
but in vain,
it's enough to look at us.[4]

IV

Les personnes faibles ne peuvent être sincères.[5]

J. R. Ackerley lived the double life – and if this was so simply because of historical circumstances it should not allow us to overlook the fact that his work, his writing, was dedicated in various forms to an ideal of sincerity. It takes, perhaps, a duplicitous actual existence to reinforce a yearning for a simplistic ideal authentic life. The differences which characterize his work – between, say, the fictional and the frankly autobiographical – cannot disguise the constancy of his obsession with gaol-breaking the falsifications of self. Ackerley wanted to love. The harrowing strength of his writing – and it develops in power as he ages – lies in that simple desire.

If we wonder, reading *My Father and Myself*, what exactly drove the man to confess posthumously, it might help to recall Eliot's words on the 'voice' of poetry: 'The first voice is the voice of the poet talking to himself – or to nobody'.[6] Ackerley's words exist within that paradox of the authentic writer – words communicate solitude: we are the solitary authors of our selves. Although he died in 1967 – a year before the false dawn of *les événements* and 'our time' – Ackerley's life was rooted in the profound events of the early years of this century. The sustained attack which his work makes upon the literal and metaphorical imprisonments humanity inflicts upon itself, his unwavering recognition of the cruelty and violence, unkindness and hatred, lovelessness and solitude, which disfigure our culture, arise directly from his experiences of the Great War. His work is a continuous but varied attempt to find and articulate value in a world which had emerged from that War. His own experiences of the Somme and his later capture and internment (1917) determined the particular focus of a single life upon our century's vast panorama of waste and futility. To experience his particular perverse triumph over the death of love is to be part of the multiple possible responses men made to extreme experience. His work is unique and thus representative: there are only the particular lives which perished or survived each in their own ways.

V

One day, whilst sauntering along the streets, I arrested myself in the act of murmuring, half aloud, these customary syllables. In a fit of petulance I re-modelled them thus: 'I am safe – I am safe – yes – if I be not fool enough to make open confession.'[7]

Ivor Gurney, on the other hand, was fool enough to confess once too often: his countrymen interned him in 1922 and he was never released. The date seems – all things considered – grimly ironic: after all, students of our literature know about 1922.

Dayadhvam: I have heard the key
Turn in the door once and turn once only
We think of the key, each in his prison
Thinking of the key, each confirms a prison[8]

The real problem of writing about Gurney lies in accepting the case-study while appreciating the poet. That approach may have some value in so far as it can enable us to glimpse – however feebly – the extent of the wounds suffered by young men of his generation. He becomes an initially representative consciousness, a tragic variation on the well known theme of 'War writers'. But that is merely a starting point: the real importance of Gurney's work is its insistence upon the *value* of his art. That might seem obvious enough, but there is a temptation to dwell on certain kinds of writing for historical rather than moral or aesthetic reasons. Gurney's work needs to be remembered because of its brave belief in the value of the conscious and conscientious struggle – whatever the circumstances – to achieve the right form. The words are seeking their proper seemly place. The significance of his art is thus found, for example, in his attempt to render the most extreme experiences possible within highly sophisticated sonnet structures. In his poetry the terribleness of immediate life intensifies the need to venerate creation. It equally accords with his reverence for other musicians and poets in his own poems, so that we are made aware of how he insisted even more intensely upon the tradition exactly as the War became more and more awful. Each poem was an instance of the whole man fighting against the emotions and feelings which could – and in the end would – destroy him. The characteristic belief in traditional forms should not mislead us – Gurney's linguistic identity was forged out of an ambitious belief that as heir to, say, on the one hand Bach and, on the other, Whitman he was composing, in the trenches, statements of the values modern man must continue to transmit. The image anticipates so much of our twentieth-century European nightmare – the extreme confrontations of creation and destruction. His voice speaks our terrible truths: a modern voice.

VI

A modern voice: in a sense, at first sight, that judgement, on the other hand, may be not at all apposite to Edward Thomas for *The Childhood of Edward Thomas* eventually takes us back to a semi-mythic rural world remote from the constraints of urban life – a world full of 'characters' defying modernity and living within a dream of liberated self-fulfilment. But the autobiographical fragment is, in fact, an ironic preparation for the last fateful acts of Edward Thomas's life. Larkin understands one aspect of the whole of Edward Thomas's work, and its Englishness, in his commentary upon that famous private patriotic gesture recorded by Eleanor Farjeon in *Edward Thomas: The Last Four Years*:

> When asked what he was fighting for, he answered 'Literally, for this', crumbling a pinch of earth between his fingers. In consequence, the England of his poems is not a Georgian dream, but the England of 1915, of farms and men 'going out', of flowers still growing because there were no boys to pick them for their girls: from his mistaken and unlucky life there arose suddenly a serene and unquestionable climax.[9]

The Edward Thomas of 'In Memoriam (Easter, 1915)' alluded to here and selected by Larkin for *The Oxford Book of Twentieth Century Verse* is indeed representative of his description:

> The flowers left thick at nightfall in the wood
> This Eastertide call into mind the men,
> Now far from home, who, with their sweethearts, should
> Have gathered them and will do never again.[10]

But equally, the Edward Thomas of 'As the Team's Head-Brass' (also alluded to and in *The Oxford Book*) is not adequately served by the specific focus of Larkin's evaluation.

> As the team's head-brass flashed out on the turn
> The lovers disappeared into the wood.
> I sat among the boughs of the fallen elm
> That strewed the angle of the fallow, and
> Watched the plough narrowing a yellow square
> Of charlock. Every time the horses turned
> Instead of treading me down, the ploughman leaned
> Upon the handles to say or ask a word,
> About the weather, next about the war.
> Scraping the share he faced towards the wood,

And screwed along the furrow till the brass flashed
Once more.
                    The blizzard felled the elm whose crest
I sat in, by a woodpecker's round hole,
The ploughman said. 'When will they take it away?'
'When the war's over.' So the talk began –
One minute and an interval of ten,
A minute more and the same interval.
'Have you been out?' 'No.' 'And don't want to, perhaps?'
'If I could only come back again, I should.
I could spare an arm. I shouldn't want to lose
A leg. If I should lose my head, why, so,
I should want nothing more . . . . Have many gone
From here?' 'Yes.' 'Many lost?' 'Yes, a good few.
Only two teams work on the farm this year.
One of my mates is dead. The second day
In France they killed him. It was back in March,
The very night of the blizzard, too. Now if
He had stayed here we should have moved the tree.'
'And I should not have sat here. Everything
Would have been different. For it would have been
Another world.' 'Ay, and a better, though
If we could see all all might seem good.' Then
The lovers came out of the wood again:
The horses started and for the last time
I watched the clods crumble and topple over
After the ploughshare and the stumbling team.[11]

Apart from this poem's technical excellence (e.g. the metrical ambiguity of the opening line allows 'flashed out' to be stressed as spondees: the fleeting passage of experience is paradoxically emphasized while simultaneously lengthened – seemingly slowed down) it has a moral and emotional depth which could only come about in response to the terrible events of a particular historical moment while simultaneously pushing beyond it to more permanent 'real' values which must – surely? – triumph. The deeper narratives – agricultural rhythms identified within the seasons: the swell and fall of the lovers in and out of the woods – these shall be our hope. Except, of course, for the poet:

The horses started and for the last time

I watched the clods crumble and topple over
After the ploughshare and the stumbling team.

Exactly: for the *last* time.

The poem exists then within its terrible contemplation of levels of determination – the night of the blizzard the tree fell, while simultaneously, in France, 'they killed him': his second day

'Now if
He had stayed here we should have moved the tree'

but then there would have been no cause to pause and sit; no conversation; no chance to see the lovers in and out of the woods and, of course, no poem. So that the triumphs of art over life are seen as illusions – perhaps necessary ('if we could see all all might seem good') – that confront the certainties of absolute terminations. And that truth about the individual consciousness and its will lies at the heart of serious English writing in our century. The creative act – what other point can there be to writing 'As the team's head-brass'? – takes place within the experience of mass suffering: it becomes the only possible assertion of the value individual lives must achieve. The tragic animus of English writing springs from this belief that individual consciousness, even as it acknowledges its end in a mass whose control lies beyond its single will, must assert its particular transient value.

VII

In Time of 'The Breaking of Nations'

I

Only a man harrowing clods
In a slow silent walk
With an old horse that stumbles and nods
Half asleep as they stalk.

II

Only thin smoke without flame
From the heaps of couch-grass;

Yet this will go onward the same
Though Dynasties pass.

III

Yonder a maid and her wight
Come whispering by:
War's annals will cloud into night
Ere their story die.[12]

Hardy's poem and 'As the Team's Head-Brass' were published in
the same year, 1917, the year of Third Ypres. And although we
might want to dwell on the similarities between the two poems this
should not distract our attention from the much more important differences. Hardy's poem is an example of his '"faculty . . . for burying
an emotion in my heart or brain for forty years and exhuming it
at the end of that time as fresh as when interred"',[13] which means
that the poem was occasioned by the Franco-Prussian War and
is an example of emotion recollected in anxiety, perhaps, but
nonetheless recollected, brought forth from the deeps of memory.
There is a subsumption of personal experience within the abstracted
figures in this poem; a disengagement (which is the source of its
optimism) impossible for Edward Thomas. The point of Hardy's
irony – it seems to have been a time of the breaking of nations
from Jeremiah on yet, somehow, through love and work, somehow
we survive – depends upon its overt historical objectivity. To contemplate the isolation of a single life in Hardy's poem would be
to misconstrue its meaning. But Edward Thomas exists *within* his
own poem; the historical moment is his and – at a level which
the poem can hardly bring itself to contemplate – grotesquely his
alone: 'Have you been out?' 'No'. 'And don't want to, perhaps?'
The consciousness of the 'I' tries, through the very act of the poem
itself, to find that courage necessary to contemplate its particular
life wracked in its own particularity.

VIII

'Marginal men' – I have appropriated this term from the sociolo-
gists. It derives from the concept of the 'stranger' as developed by

Georg Simmel. The 'stranger' is the wanderer who 'comes today and stays tomorrow'.

> He is fixed within a certain spatial circle ... but his position within it is fundamentally affected by the fact that he does not belong in it initially and that he brings qualities into it that are not, and cannot be, indigenous to it.[14]

The consequence is paradoxical: the stranger is both an inauthentic member of the group - Simmel observes that his prototype is the trader, specifically the Jewish merchant, rootless and without land – and a figure of curiously compelling power.

> Because he is not bound by roots to the particular constituents and partisan dispositions of the group, he confronts all of these with a distinctly 'objective' attitude, an attitude that does not signify mere detachment and nonparticipation, but is a distinct structure composed of remoteness and nearness, indifference and involvement.[15]

Developing Simmel's original concept, the American sociologist Robert E. Park introduced the term 'marginal man' in 1928. Park's particular use[16] of Simmel's original essay need not detain us (although the variation effected by Park upon the Jew has curious resonance: 'his idealism and lack of historical sense, are the characteristics of the city man, the man who ranges widely, lives preferably in a hotel – in short, the cosmopolite'[17]), since his specific interest in the concept of strangeness was directed towards the transformations of early twentieth century American urban life. Nonetheless the phrase itself – 'marginal man' – and its roots in Simmel's original essay 'Der Fremde' are of considerable use when applied to the development of English writing in this century.

Simmel observes – brilliantly – that the stranger's *objectivity* is at the heart of his curious presence; indeed in extreme circumstances the stranger may receive from members of the community he enters 'most surprising revelations and confidences, at times reminiscent of a confessional, about matters which are kept hidden from everybody with whom one is close'.[18] Objectivity, Simmel insists, thus is not a failure to participate; rather it is a lack of prejudice, of *parti pris*, creating a mind which is free; it can speak in ways not possible for a member of the community.

Turn this concept upon twentieth-century English writing and
certain distinct configurations become clear. Into the pre-War English literary community enter the strangers – James, Conrad, Pound,
Eliot. These figures become, in time, central voices of English writing; indeed, in the case of (temporarily) Pound and (permanently)
Eliot, they seem to become rapidly and out of all proportion the
central prophetic voices of the age. Even if we allow some degree
of exaggeration in such a narrative, the career of Eliot, for example,
nonetheless accords precisely with the 'stranger' hypothesis. His
power as an observer and later, as an Englishman, participant in
his new culture comes from his presumed *objectivity*. He is free to
judge his new culture, assert its 'true' values and even introduce
dimensions of alien cultures – with which, of necessity, he is familiar – to his trusting hosts. And indeed it is no accident therefore
that so much emphasis should be laid upon theories of objectivity
by the stranger himself: objective correlatives, impersonal theories
of poetry, scientific analogies, tradition itself, all sustain the very
ideals of which, as the stranger, he himself is an embodiment. And,
of course, as Simmel observes, as objective *listener* the stranger is
party to the confessions of others – he himself remains silent up to
a point:

> 'My nerves are bad to-night. Yes, bad. Stay with me.
> 'Speak to me. Why do you never speak. Speak.
> 'What are you thinking of? What thinking? What?
> 'I never know what you are thinking. Think.'[19]

I read, much of the night, and go south in the winter.[20]

But there is one crucial aspect of our stranger which calls for
a modification to Simmel's description. Ironically, the objective
disinterested listener is further free to reveal his own prejudices
fostered in the culture which spawned him. And in the case of, for
example, Eliot, there were strong prejudices indeed about, of course,
the stranger. Who knows what depths of self-analysis are ironically
revealed as the original American stranger, Park's 'marginal man',
re-emerges in Eliot's writing? Now the very strangeness of the
stranger makes *his* models of the stranger even more compelling:
his objective status assures the hosts that there must indeed be
something unspeakable about these shadowy cosmopolitans in
hotel rooms:

> Unreal City
> Under the brown fog of a winter noon
> Mr Eugenides, the Smyrna merchant
> Unshaven, with a pocket full of currants
> C.i.f. London: documents at sight,
> Asked me in demotic French
> To luncheon at the Cannon Street Hotel
> Followed by a weekend at the Metropole.[21]

The models of a 'mélange adultère de tout' – 'Chicago Semite Viennese' – are sardonic and degrading mirror-images of himself: objectifying himself thus the stranger paradoxically *reinforces* his self-normalisation. The focus of otherness, of the alien, is transposed and, ironically, the detached normative status of the stranger is re-inforced:

> And the Jew squats on the window sill, the owner,
> Spawned in some estaminet of Antwerp,
> Blistered in Brussels, patched and peeled in London.[22]

So the stranger adopts and adapts the alien culture; absorbing his new milieu he becomes increasingly a figure of authority – he has chosen us – and is able now to speak in that voice which indeed declares its authenticity:

> Because I do not hope to turn again
> Because I do not hope
> Because I do not hope to turn
> Desiring this man's gift and that man's scope
> I no longer strive to strive towards such things[23]

The revision of Shakespeare's words (among others') here is an assertion of the complete authoritative identity:

> I all alone beweep my outcast state[24]

IX

Into this context of the stranger and his own concept of strangeness can now be introduced the appropriated and redefined concept of

'marginal men'. It is essential to the profound effect 'Modernist' strangers had upon English culture that they arrived at a
moment of historical crisis: the Great War. Simmel's observation
about the possibility of 'objectivity' becomes even more fruitful
in this context. If men like Edward Thomas, Ivor Gurney and
J. R. Ackerley were traumatized in a variety of ways – their writing
essentially transformed by the experiences of anticipating death,
suffering wounds and incarceration – that fact both particularizes
and generalizes their experience. The suffering is unique – or the
response to it: the experiences are of the mass. But upon Eliot – the
American neutral – pressed quite other considerations. Here he is
writing to his mother in October 1917; the disaster of Ypres is well
under way:

> So I shall have my hands just as full as I expected; and it is a
> good thing to be so busy that one cannot take time to worry
> much about the present condition of the world and the future
> of civilization. Also I take a great deal of pleasure in *The Egoist*;
> struggling as it is, it is known to some of the most intelligent
> people, and it stands for something which needs to be kept going;
> the fact that it is practically the only publication, except perhaps
> technical ones, which makes no reference to politics or the war,
> and that it can keep on its way determined to assert the perpetual
> importance of other things, is itself important; even though it is
> possible to get only a small number of the good contributors who
> were possible a few years ago. I ought to be pretty well satisfied
> with my life then, in a way, seeing that I can name almost no one
> whose life has not been thoroughly disorganised in the last three
> years.[25]

The point here may not be *necessarily* judgemental – why indeed
should Eliot have considered any course of action other than that of
sustaining the culture he had adopted? The point concerns rather the
paradox of the stranger (and Eliot in his letters refers to himself as
such) who, in a crisis, is able to select and 'objectively' deem what
values are worth preserving. He becomes an important – indeed
a normative – figure as the culture welcomes his presence: his
very arbitrariness becomes part of the mystical rightness of that
presence.

The final step in this description, then, is obvious. The stranger paradoxically becomes the example of a dominant voice – the normative consciousness. For, the natives of his adopted culture – here his literary peers (nota bene the importance of their youthfulness: the *future* of the culture is at risk) – perforce have had to leave their homes to fight in a foreign land and act out their historical roles as threatened sons defending their own soil, their own language. When the natives return they do so *not* simply as the returning sons of the soil, nor as their apparent diametric opposite, the stranger, but as something quite different, a third category of being – the estranged. The once native is now a new creature – the 'marginal man'. His only true peers are other soldiers: within his own culture, he returns to see himself in all the different forms of exile that are possible. Pushed to the edges, he is an alienated consciousness, marginalized by the very culture he fought to save. The stranger now exists at the middle, articulating objectively the values he has understood to be worth saving; the marginalized native exists in a limbo creatively: he has too much to tell of destruction and terror, too much of all that is not to be preserved in the pages of *The Egoist*. If the theme of exile became central in 'Modernist' writing, it was the exile of the cosmopolitan stranger. The voices displaced – the voices of the native sons – are actually more profoundly alienated; exiled from the supposed centres of cosmopolitan literary consciousness. Thus the paradox is complete: *English* English writing comes to be seen as somehow provincial, at the edges because it lacks the objective centrality determined by the stranger. 'The good little Thomas Hardy' – James's notorious remark (passed down with approval by Leavis in *The Great Tradition* as 'the appropriately sympathetic note'[26]) appropriately establishes the tone.

And so deep is this marginalization – at times dimly perceived, or at best half understood even by the most important observers of English culture[27] – that it survives and finds articulation in writers who have had no direct experience of the Great War; survives in distorted but utterly valid forms within voices of contemporary reaction. That it should be deemed necessary by Philip Larkin to draw upon strangely felt resources of hostility in order to validate his rejection of Eliot, say, is of profound significance today. Here is a writer in our time aware of not just a personal estrangement – for that there is no accounting, apart from recognizing its difficult particularity – but also a deeper sense of malaise and exile within the very culture, the very language, he seeks to celebrate.

Rather than words comes the thought of high windows[28]

It may get you, in the end, a service at Westminster Abbey, but the poet whom the established culture was honouring could write this;

> In shoeless corridors, the lights burn. How
> Isolated, like a fort, it is –
> The headed paper, made for writing home
> (If home existed) letters of exile: *Now*
> *Night comes on. Waves fold behind villages.*[29]

because, among other things, he had thought about the significance and consequences of this:

MCMXIV

> Those long uneven lines
> Standing as patiently
> As if they were stretched outside
> The Oval or Villa Park,
> The crowns of hats, the sun
> On moustached archaic faces
> Grinning as if it were all
> An August Bank Holiday lark;
>
> And the shut shops, the bleached
> Established names on the sunblinds,
> The farthings and sovereigns,
> And dark-clothed children at play
> Called after kings and queens,
> The tin advertisements
> For cocoa and twist, and the pubs
> Wide open all day;
>
> And the countryside not caring:
> The place-names all hazed over
> With flowering grasses, and fields
> Shadowing Domesday lines
> Under wheat's restless silence;
> The differently-dressed servants

With tiny rooms in huge houses,
The dust behind limousines;

Never such innocence,
Never before or since,
As changed itself to past
Without a word – the men
Leaving the gardens tidy,
The thousands of marriages
Lasting a little while longer:
Never such innocence again.[30]

1

The Childhood
of Edward Thomas

'Only I can't help wishing he could have saved his life without so wholly losing it. . .'[1]

'I could also enjoy kinds of fighting where it was impossible to think of poetry.'[2]

Towards the end of 1913 Edward Thomas wrote this: 'When I penetrate backward into my childhood I come perhaps sooner than many people to impassable night. A sweet darkness enfolds with a faint blessing my life up to the age of about four. The task of attempting stubbornly to break up that darkness is one I have never proposed to myself, but I have many times gone up to the edge of it, peering, listening, stretching out my hands . . .' These curious sentences make up the opening of the autobiographical fragment which now bears the title *The Childhood of Edward Thomas*. It was not published until 1938 – twenty-one years after Thomas was killed at Arras:

> With regard to his actual death you have probably heard the details. It should be of some comfort to you to know that he died at a moment of victory from a direct hit by a shell, which must have killed him outright without giving him a chance to realise anything, – a gallant death for a very true and gallant gentleman.
>
> We buried him in a little military cemetery a few hundred yards from the battery: the exact spot will be notified to you by the parson. As we stood by the grave the sun came and the guns round seemed to stop firing for a short time. This typified to me what stood out most in your husband's character – the spirit of quiet, sunny, unassuming cheerfulness.

He was – Captain Lushington recalled – 'rather older than most of the officers and we all looked up to him as the kind father of our happy family'.[3] But the truth of the matter is that these attempts to make the unbearable bearable lead us away from the recorded reality of the man; for if Edward Thomas did appear to find some kind of contentment in his war-time 'family' it must have been a satisfaction quite against the apparent grain: his own father he wrote off thus:

> I may come near loving you
> When you are dead
> And there is nothing to do
> And much to be said.
>
> . . .
>
> But not so long as you live
> Can I love you at all.[4]

About his own family he wrote more tortuously; as in the following poem, one of three bearing the title – most significantly as we shall see – of 'Home':

> Fair was the morning, fair our tempers, and
> We had seen nothing fairer than that land,
> Though strange, and the untrodden snow that made
> Wild of the tame, casting out all that was
> Not wild and rustic and old; and we were glad.
>
> Fair too was afternoon, and first to pass
> Were we that league of snow, next the north wind.
>
> There was nothing to return for except need.
> And yet we sang nor ever stopped for speed,
> As we did often with the start behind.
> Faster still strode we when we came in sight
> Of the cold roofs where we must spend the night.
>
> Happy we had not been there, nor could be,
> Though we had tasted sleep and food and fellowship
> Together long.
>   'How quick' to someone's lip
> The word came, 'will the beaten horse run home.'
>
> The word 'home' raised a smile in us all three,

And one repeated it, smiling just so
That all knew what he meant and none would say.
Between three counties far apart that lay
We were divided and looked strangely each
At the other, and we knew we were not friends
But fellows in a union that ends
With the necessity for it, as it ought.

Never a word was spoken, not a thought
Was thought, of what the look meant with the word
'Home' as we walked and watched the sunset blurred.
And then to me the word, only the word,
'Homesick', as it were playfully occurred:
No more. If I should ever more admit
Than the mere word I could not endure it
For a day longer: this captivity
Must somehow come to an end, else I should be
Another man, as often now I seem,
Or this life be only an evil dream. [5]

'Homesick': the word becomes the hinge round which the mind
swings back into or out away from the space (mental and material)
which contains all one is meant to love. The sickness is both of
and for the home; appropriately the poem's ending sustains the
confusion – the schizophrenic 'escape' out of the captivity which
keeps Edward Thomas away from home, or the captivity which *is*
that very home itself, can only be resolved by creating 'another man'
to escape from the 'evil dream' which either is or is not the existence
circumscribed by the single word – 'home'. There are several ways
in which one is a captive of – hostage to – one's own creation: the
house; the family within that house; the home; the *poem* of the home.
For behind – no: within – the writing itself is a highly developed
sense of self-hatred which the act of creation only intensifies. For
it is the case with Edward Thomas that we have a portrait of the
artist as a doomed man; a man for whom the word becomes both
the instrument of torture and the tool of escape. It is both the
material reality and a sardonic commentary upon that devastating
fact. When you are the hack from whose shelter the poet refuses
for most of his life to escape, self-criticism will surely seek to state
its reservations in the 'disease' of 'self-contempt' – to use Edward
Thomas's own words.[6] And here we have the paradox of Edward

Thomas: his life is inseparable from the act of writing; but it is only when in turn the act becomes a protest against such a life that he can contemplate escape. Escape, however, takes many different and sometimes unvirtuous forms.

For Edward Thomas material existence had to be supported by hack-work. In 1911 he was working on six books simultaneously: not surprisingly therefore financial worries and ill-health through overwork brought on a severe nervous breakdown. So the act of writing and reviewing, of writing about and reviewing other people and other people's books, is both necessary and futile. There is no escape from this labour: the sacrifice is for a wife and children and with that feeling always present – something of the self being sacrificed – can only come resentment at best or despair at worst. That is why in Edward Thomas's case writing *for* himself – writing selfishly, meanly – becomes a necessary act of negative liberation. He writes poetry to destroy the other writer – the hack: the act of creation is *au fond* an act of violence.

The centre of Edward Thomas's working life is therefore occupied by a chimera – a liberated self which can only grow out of the destruction of the other, the responsible loving father and husband. Ultimately – as we shall see – the condition of absence has to displace the 'normal' human emotions and responses. Edward Thomas's life becomes then a preparation for the return to that 'sweet darkness' out of which it emerged into painful consciousness. Killing is therefore the ultimate act of liberation for him; killing his self and so his old life – as he obliquely realizes in his autobiography – becomes a preparation for that act.

II

'Homesick' – with the cognates 'nostalgic' the word can imply a degree of inadequacy before the facts of adult life; a debilitation in the face of the present and – arguably – a fear of the future. To this extent the emotions suggested by the words seek resolution in flight – escape into the past. This point is taken from D. W. Harding's 'Note on Nostalgia' in *Scrutiny* where he observes that the nostalgia which 'pervades' Edward Thomas's poetry is subtly bound up with powerful regressive tendencies; nostalgia implies a yearning for – ultimately – the conditions of childhood and so flight from the unsympathetic 'social group' within which one is trapped.[7] However, adult life becomes horribly complicated if the unsatisfactory 'social group' in question is not – say – hostile bourgeois society (*vide* Lawrence) but *one's own created family*. Thus the home may not only fail to provide the support for which the self yearns, it can actually produce an environment in which an unsuccessful provider might feel deeply contemptuous of himself. The tragic paradox of being a stranger in one's own house has its classic expression, of course, with 'Frost at Midnight'.

Given all this, it seems – nonetheless – that Harding's account of 'nostalgia' is not sufficiently comprehensive to account for our reactions to – say – the poem with which we started, 'Home'. Part of that inadequacy lies in the fact that Edward Thomas is always ahead of us – as it were; he knows the price to be paid if the word 'homesick' becomes more than 'the word, only the word'. For if that happens then it has to be understood that the group to which he is returning – the family – is the source of his weakness; he is ensnared by it and cannot bear its absence. He feels both inadequate within it and impotent without it.

If we return to the poem's beginning we can now realize how strongly its conclusion is running away from that which Edward Thomas wants to want – namely an aggressive, animalistic freedom which is elemental and utterly hostile to ideas of civilization and home: hence the repetitions of the word 'wild'. And hence – equally – its laconic opposite, 'need' ('There was nothing to return for except need') suggesting excuse rather than explanation. The poem is thus a bitter comment on the need to run away from Freedom; to seek home, to become a crippled prisoner of – and here is the twist – an environment from which one ran away in the first place.

'In most of the poems there is no recognition of an underlying social cause for his feeling'.[8] Harding's judgement here must be with Lawrence – by contrast – in mind. And it certainly would seem to be true in 'Home' that the point of dissatisfaction is made without any specific *j'accuse* as its cause; but to limit ourselves to a culpable society – with all its complicated relations – *out there* is to mistake the force of Edward Thomas's writing and – above all – its distressing honesty. For in his work the 'social cause' is to be found in the very act of writing itself. In writing the *poem* 'Home' he is actually wasting time by working on, making, a thing which is materially useless, unable to sustain the 'home'.

But even if the poem is a literal rejection of functional writing, it won't do to imagine that the relations between poet and hack are to be balanced around freedom and responsibility; indeed, the poet was the hack's only begetter. For it is the ironic truth of Edward Thomas's life that the very roots of his life's evil dream can be traced back to that moment of his early adult experience when he appeared to have miraculously got it right, the poise between intellectual freedom – writing – and social recognition – more – love. It was through his teenage love affair with Helen Noble that Edward Thomas came to know her father who, as a minor man of London letters, became a patron by helping the precocious young man get a number of essays published in established literary magazines. As the affair became more obviously serious, Helen Noble's mother made the classic parental blunder of forbidding her daughter to have any further dealings with the young 'author' and so the business had a Lawrentian aura to it: Edward Thomas became a real-life Paul Morel. At the age of nineteen he went up to Oxford with a published book – *The Woodland Life* – and a mistress. Helen Noble describes the consummation:

> Then I held out my hands to him – for he was standing now, and he raised me to my feet, so that my clothes slid down in a ring. I stepped out of them on to the soft moss and dry leaves, and he kneeling kissed my body from my feet up to my knees, and from my knees up to my hips, and when he had kissed me and let his hand wander all over me he laid me down on the moss, and I lay with my eyes closed, just conscious that he was quickly undressing, and hearing his voice speaking some passionate name. And I knowing he was ready, opened my eyes and saw him standing there naked, said 'Come', and drew him to my breast.[9]

Clapham Common became the Garden of Eden – true; but it was mere nature which eventually decided things as Edward Thomas was transformed from the Romantic young writer who actually possessed his own Fanny Brawne into just another undergraduate father-to-be and finally newly-graduated father with little Merfyn and his mother to support. And how else to do that but by the thing at which he was best – writing? The record of that life as related by Helen Thomas in *World Without End* is deeply distressing. There is no Romantic passion in their shared misery but a kind of grinding domestic servitude on her part to the love and loyalty of home which could only be reciprocated by her husband's mechanical repetition of materially 'meaningful' words. To write out of this *for* this was, in a sense, to be poisoned by the very thing you love. His whole life and hers had become an ironic jest – a tale of romantic fiction mocked by a nightmare of words seeking their reward. But not to be commissioned – not to write – was obviously the worst. Helen Thomas recalls the experience of failure in bitter detail:

> I sat down on the hedge bank, and taking him in my arms mixed my tears with his and bending over him tried to sing his favourite good-night songs to comfort him and stop his sobs. A little bunch of the flowers growing within reach and a feather found on the thorn soon comforted him, and he forgot as I shall never forget that dreadful morning.
>
> I put Philip to bed before going to the study where I found David [i.e. Edward Thomas] sitting as I had left him, not reading, not smoking, with his head in his hands, staring with eyes that saw nothing.
>
> 'There are no letters.'
>
> 'Why tell me what is written on your pale wretched face? I am cursed, and you are cursed because of me. I hate the tears I see you've been crying. Your sympathy and your love are both hateful to me. Hate me, but for God's sake don't stand there, pale and suffering. Leave me, I tell you; get out and leave me.' [10]

And Edward Thomas himself reduced some part of it to miserable empty absurdity most terribly in 'The long small room':

> The long small room that showed willows in the west
> Narrowed up to the end the fireplace filled,
> Although not wide. I liked it. No one guessed
> What need or accident made them so build.
>
> Only the moon, the mouse and the sparrow peeped
> In from the ivy round the casement thick.
> Of all they saw and heard there they shall keep
> The tale for the old ivy and older brick.
>
> When I look back I am like moon, sparrow and mouse
> That witnessed what they could never understand
> Or alter or prevent in the dark house.

One thing remains the same – this my right hand

Crawling crab-like over the clean white page,
Resting awhile each morning on the pillow,
Then once more starting to crawl on towards age.
The hundred last leaves stream upon the willow.[11]

It seems fair to say that the progress of this poem is, as it were, backwards; that we have a clear example of 'nostalgic' writing – until the last stanza, of course. The regressive emotions that lie at the poem's centre are, however, necessary to its *dénouement*; for there is much play with the idea of not being 'grown-up' in the main body of the poem. The sense of 'childishness' is evoked through the assertion of moods and likes without any justification or explanation: 'Although not wide. I liked it. No one guessed/ What need or accident made them so build.' If we are not yet clear that this is actually the language of escape, it becomes obvious in the next two stanzas as the words conjure in the mind's eye a scene from Beatrix Potter. The verb of adult retrospection is displaced by the coyness of 'peeped', uniting – as it comfortably does – moon, mouse, sparrow and ivy in a friendly approach, as it were, to the childish bed; a dream of the child's dream. The regression here is much more overt than in 'Home' and, if anything, more apparently contemptible. For here there is an insistence upon impotence; the adult excuses his feebleness by assuming the right to childish helplessness:

When I look back I am like moon, sparrow and mouse
That witnessed what they could never understand
Or alter or prevent in the dark house.

Up to this moment the reader has been happily superior to the poem's development within the category of 'nostalgic' writing; but even as we condescend to its regression Edward Thomas is preparing to drag us towards adult truths of the most unpleasant kind:

One thing remains the same – this my right hand

Crawling crab-like over the clean white page.

Writing: the poem is about the adult Edward Thomas and his condition; the nightmare of the writer. The middle of the poem is, then, part of this cruel irony; the regressive centre is, after all, only possible within *adult* consciousness so that even as Edward Thomas remembers his earlier life in terms of a 'nostalgic' language (moon, sparrow, mouse) he is aware that he lived then as he does now – i.e. at the moment of writing the poem: nothing more than (in an ironic recapitulation of the language of diminution) a 'right hand'. The stanza break offered the illusion of time and space separating past from present even as the words conveyed the opposite message – 'one thing remains the same'. So that to write 'nostalgically' is indeed to imprison oneself – it is after all still to *write*. And to write about that writing is to encircle one's own impotence within a hard logic of self-analysis. There is no story then other than the story that there is no story and that one goes on as one can writing meaninglessly until death. So what's the news? Only this: that the poem is nevertheless – for good or ill – simply that: a poem. It is something other and we are made conscious of this by its last line which seems to let us know what is at stake: 'The hundred last leaves stream upon the willow.' It is both part of that which preceded it and yet utterly independent; isolated from and yet tied back into the poem through its very first line. It may be that the willows were part of the room's likeability – but how can we tell? All we know is that part of the right hand's Lear-like crawl towards death is its act of recording the willow's hundred last leaves in absentia. If that is an act of the imagination, it is equally such a deliberately imprecise one that we are left groping towards significance: inferring meaning. The preposition ensures uncertainty: are the leaves attached to the willow or streaming against it? Does the verb suggest the action of life streaming past in a Heraclitean flux or pathetically imply weeping? Are we meant to think across from the leaves to the pages of the right hand's books and so to the right hand itself? Finally are we illuminated by the precise enumeration – 'hundred last'?

This line is the 'real' poem; its freedom of inference plays along the edge of its half-attached Imagist relation to the rest of the verse. It has an anarchic existence which seems to be close to our sense of 'modern' poetry. If you want it to 'mean' something then you can so make it – nothing is given. In this sense – in the poem's final unaccountability, its mystery, its self-centred irresponsibility – there is both an inescapable moment in the life of a drudge and a privileged secret rejection of all that. It is necessary and irrelevant; its irrelevance we can understand but it is the immaterial necessity (why go on?) which needs explanation and that – it so happens – can be partly found in the document known as *The Childhood of Edward Thomas*.

III

The passage with which we started – the opening paragraph of *The Childhood of Edward Thomas* – continues as follows:

> . . . and I have heard the voice of one singing as I sat or lay in her arms; and I have become again aware very dimly of being enclosed in rooms that were shadowy, whether by comparison with outer sunlight I know not. The songs, first of my mother, then of her younger sister, I can hear not only afar off behind the veil but on this side of it also. I was, I should think, a very still listener whom the music flowed through and filled to the exclusion of all thought and of all sensation except of blissful easy fullness, so that too early or too sudden ceasing would have meant pangs of expectant emptiness. The one song which, by reason of its repetition or of some aptitude in me, I well remember, was one combining fondness with tranquil if peevish retrospection and regret in a soft heavy twilight. I reach back to it in that effort through a thousand twilights lineally descended from that first one and from the night which gave it birth. If I cried or suffered pain or deprivation in those years nothing remains to star the darkness. Either I asked no question or I had none but sweet answers. I was at peace with life. Indoors, out of the sun, I seem never to have been troubled by heat or cold strong enough to be remembered. [12]

Here is an evocation of warmth before, during and immediately after the emergence of consciousness which certainly suggests a post-Romantic poetic birth – in both senses. The sensitivity to sound ('a very still listener whom the music flowed through') reminds us of Eliot's tribute to De La Mare's early world with its 'inexplicable mystery of sound' and 'The whispered incantation which allows / Free passage to the phantoms of the mind'.[13]

This appeal to the 'dark years' and their aural intensity sets up a first emergence into light with an odd negative inclusiveness – 'But out of doors, somewhere at the verge of the dark years . . . I lay in the tall grass and buttercups of a narrow field at the edge of London and saw the sky and nothing but the sky'[14] – giving us all and nothing, so disposing us to think again in terms of regressive writing. Here – despite the pleasure of solitude and sky – is the first world, the world of pre-natal darkness: that first remembered song combined 'fondness with tranquil if peevish retrospection and regret in a soft heavy twilight' – the first of a thousand 'twilights lineally descended'.

If the fragment were to continue in this manner for long we might soon weary of its sombre grandeur, bored by its melancholic undertone so much a part of 'nostalgic' writing. Not even connections with the poetry's obsessive desire for the peace of darkness (an absoluteness – in fact – for death) would allow the prose a significant life of its own. But the next paragraph breaks away from these opaque beginnings and sends us mundanely forth into the world of 'normal' childhood: 'Then I entered the lowest class of a large suburban board school.' What follows is a laconic account of growing up in turn-of-the-century London which develops rapidly into a masterpiece of subversive literature.

The context of its recollections is – perhaps – at first unpromising: Battersea, Wandsworth, Clapham seem solid enough. True, there were mean streets south of the river, but Edward Thomas was safely raised in the genteel comfort of the minor civil servant's house with domestics and Sunday lunches. No – it was the position of the area on the *margin* of Dickensian London which is important; what mattered were not just the childhood streets and all their dangers but even more the great suburban parks and Commons at Battersea, Wandsworth and Clapham; these were the wild rural woods and untamed downs of the real countryside. Here a boy could find himself:

The ponds were for paddling in. One of them, a shallow irregular one, weedy and rushy-margined, lying then in some broken ground between the Three Island and the railway, was full of effets and frogs. Bigger boys would torture the frogs, by cutting, skinning or crushing them alive. The sharp penknives sank through the skin and the soft bone into the wood of the seat which was the operating table. This seat and earth under and about it would be strewn with fragments, pale bellies slit up, and complete frogs seeming to be munching their own insides. At that time I could not have done it myself, but my horror lacked pity and turned into a kind of half-shrinking, half-gloating curiosity.[15]

This passage is typical both of the fragment's content and its narrative rhythm: the mind drifts across the landscape until it stops to dwell, with detached fascination, upon cruelty and suffering, torture and death. The world of children is seen as embedded in brutality: games merge into battles; play is a form of conflict. It is 'normal', moreover, to discover oneself in a world characterized by the violence of humans upon animals; in the book's opening chapter – 'Infancy' – Edward Thomas's first anecdote concerns a mad dog hiding in a garden; a man takes up a pickaxe: 'I do not know that I saw the blow struck, but the idea of sharp heavy steel piercing the shaggy hair, flesh and bone of a living creature has remained horrible and ineffaceable ever since'.[16] And this is the central theme of this 'absurd total' of recollections.[17] At first the violence appears to be indiscriminate, for it is one of the fragment's mysterious qualities to refuse the conventions of any narrative which might suggest a guided development of the self. Incidents happen, events take place, but no purpose is ever suggested; no guidance is ever laid down. Instead a pattern emerges among the different kinds of violence the autobiography records, which sardonically reveals the truth of the man who descends from them.

One extreme of the anecdotal spectrum centres upon those acts of 'excusable' violence which human beings explain in terms of survival; there is the moment in the slaughter house when the child finds out how to kill a cow:

> The tall pale butcher came along, shoved her a little sideways to get her perfectly into position, and brought down the pointed knob of the poleaxe smartly upon her forehead. The rope was slackened, she fell heavily. The man thrust a cane into the opening in the forehead, 'to stir the brains', said my fellow watcher. The butcher cut her throat and the blood rattled into a bucket, while the man stood, with one foot on the ground clear of her gesticulating legs, and one upon her flank, working it up and down to help the blood out. . . [18]

The reminiscence closes with the confession that the 'only physical pain I could myself inflict with pleasure was upon fish'; and this becomes the opening for a new set of variations upon the techniques of slaughter:

And there were several ways of destroying a little fish. For example, I could stamp it violently out of existence. Or I could break its head off. Gradually I found myself mildly enjoying the act of driving my thumb-nail through the neck or into the back in several places. The body quivered violently; but no sound was made, nor did the eyes express anything. If the root of the tail was squeezed hard between two finger-nails the quivering went on for a long time. Several times I forced the bladder out of the body. But these were isolated brief pleasures. I did nothing else of the sort. I never intentionally tortured an animal, though I did protract the drowning of a cat by putting it into a copper that had not been quite filled: as I sat on the lid I sang street tunes very loudly to hide the sounds within and to keep up my courage. I hated having to kill a wounded pigeon. Nevertheless I did it, with a beating heart. When I killed my first snake – it was in reality a blind-worm – I stabbed it so frenziedly that I was lucky not to hurt myself; the frenzy being due partly to suppressed fear, partly to the novelty. As to fish, I very soon began to pride myself on killing what I caught instead of throwing it into the hedge behind, as the factory men usually did, there to die slowly. Pressing the under jaw of the jack against a stone I bent his long body up and over until his neck was broken and his back met his upper jaw. With a smaller fish I inserted the two first fingers into the gills and forced back the head until it was loose. I think that care and pride in doing this neatly and swiftly obliterated any mere pleasure in pain, though it was, I think, accompanied by a slight suffocation and beating of the heart and clouding of the brain. [19]

Although the minor parallels to the anecdote of the slaughterhouse suggest dispassionate reportage, it is the extra-dimension of personal sensations, calmly related, harmonizing the experiences of killing, which disturbs: 'I found myself mildly enjoying the act of driving my thumb-nail through the neck . . .'; 'But these were isolated brief pleasures . . .'; 'though I did protract the drowning of a cat . . .'; 'When I killed my first snake I stabbed it so frenziedly . . .'; 'As to fish, I very soon began to pride myself on killing what I caught . . .'; all of which leads up to the conjunction of professional self-regard – 'that care and pride in doing this swiftly and neatly' – with personal reaction: 'slight suffocation and beating of the heart and clouding of the brain'. Act and reaction are there – what we lack is the guidance of an 'and therefore', and 'I came to realize'. It may not even be amoral distancing we seek but simply a narrative control. In the course of reading such recollections we forget the man behind the pen in any other existence than as amanuensis. 'These things happened'. And then? 'And then these other things happened'.

These anecdotes exist simultaneously at extremes of the spectrum. Their force lies in the fact that they are seen as both 'normal' and – as in the parodistic catalogue of the child's own memories of killing – abhorrent. None the less, both in adults and children, they expose the centre of life. Equally, another anecdote starts off within that centrality and casually turns itself into a moral fable without judgement. The boy becomes a pigeon-fancier; his particular desire is for a pair of young black-chequers; long-distance homers:

> I was to have them, so I understood, for two-and-six the pair. When I already had them in my hand I learnt they were two-and-six each. This was beyond my means, nor did I want to have one of them at such a price. So he took them back into his hands at the door. Then while I was still lingering he put the head of one bird in his mouth, as I imagined in fun, or to slip a grain into its beak. His teeth closed on the slender neck tighter and tighter, the wings flapped and quivered, and when he opened his jaws the bird was dead. I was speechless, on the edge of tears. He looked down at me with a half-pitying grin, remarking that I was 'still soft-hearted'. My tenderness turned to hatred for the man, yet I could not speak. I dared not show my feeling. With only a meek resentfulness I even accepted his gift of the surviving bird. It became the prize of my pigeon house, always distinguished as 'the young homer'. The man I never did more than nod to again. [20]

In that nod, presumably, lies the point of the story: the gesture remains indecipherable – is it a sign of contempt, gratitude, pride, obeisance? – except as a recognition by the child of the one fact of adult life: compromise. The truth of these 'absurd' memories is in their laconic evocation of 'normal' experience, of civilisation in all its savage hypocrisy. Violence is necessary even when it is gratuitous – that is the fact of the boy's moral education.

Except that there is a whole other to the autobiography which takes that cruel truth and reworks it so that it is seen *as a truth*; this, in turn, becomes an honesty about life which is at the amoral

centre of a genuine anarchic counter-culture; one to which Edward
Thomas would – if he could – have truly belonged.

The older Thomases were dissenters – Liberal/Labour in politics,
Chapel in religion – but sufficiently (egregiously indeed) bourgeois
to give the boy something from which to escape. The flight from
home began early. For it was to a world beyond the Common, to
the West Country – Wiltshire – that he gave his soul away. Here
he found himself savagely free; here he revelled in a criminal
indifference to the laws of propriety and sensibility; here the child
was no longer impotent before the bully; here he could be a part of
the poacher's culture. It is in Wiltshire that the autobiography finds
its heroes: first the Uncle who '[w]ith a jaunty laugh deprecating my
grandmother's tears and blessings and my aunt's fierce distress,
with a sixpenny bit for my brother and me' strode out of the home
'which can have had little charm for him' and disappeared to South
Africa.[21] From this man and his peers Edward Thomas learned the
'truth' of amorality – its utter careless stupid freedom:

> But the chief Sunday sport was with water rats. We were fasci-
> nated as men yelled encouragements, threats, advice, or praises,
> and a terrier swam down a rat in spite of its divings. When no
> dog was handy a rat surprised in mid-stream was a good mark
> for a stone, a snake's head a more difficult one. The moorhens in
> the reeds had no more mercy from them, but more often than not
> escaped. A dead dog was a good deal better than nothing. Not
> that we were unhappy without something for a mark. We threw
> flat stones to make ducks and drakes along the sunny water, or
> sheltering from rain under one of the low stone bridges plunged
> heavy stones with all our might down into the black depth . . .
> Perhaps it was a little later that I first went out fishing with
> my uncle. He had not the patience of a fisherman. But there was
> nothing he did not know: the very winch that he used was made
> in the factory surreptitiously. He caught roach, and before long I
> followed him. Even better than this was the sport of seeing him
> confound the water bailiff who asked for his licence. What with
> gay lies, chaff and threats, the man had to go. We feared nothing
> at my uncle's side. [22]

The figure of the poacher, the moucher, is the hero not just of childhood – and as we shall see the father to the man is forerunner to
the tragic – but in adulthood also. These men stood before the child

as visions of a future that would eliminate all of daily rectitude's impediments to freedom. In Swindon, Edward Thomas found his Freds and Dads – men who would 'do almost anything to please me, from fishing with me all day, to killing a neighbour's cat for me to skin'.[23] These are men who imitate bird songs, know all the flowers, know the paths to the best rat-shooting, have the most powerful catapults, the best fishing sense, the best nose for nests – knew the woods as their home. Among these rural deviants are found honesty and freedom; with men such as Dad – who appeared 'wicked' until one came to realise that 'all men were radically like him but most of them inferior in honesty'[24] – for 'the most part we were moving and usually fast'.[25] Honest rapid movers: the child could travel through a real fantasy world as one of the rogues, the rural petty criminals. *The Childhood* presents an Edward Thomas who constantly creates a recollected self which lives on the edge of a real rebellion against convention – but never heroically. He is a truly English spirit; the boy who 'habitually told the truth when [there was] nothing which [he] thought could easily be gained by lying';[26] who was deceitful but in dread of it; who sneaked on a boy cheating at his examinations; who 'discovered the joy of throwing stones over into the unknown depths of a great garden and hearing the glass-house break'.[27] This is the true spirit of Wiltshire which sustains him on his return to London:

Even the way home from school held its adventures. There was, for instance, a fight with a schoolfellow who gave me once for all the felicity of holding him round the neck with one arm while I punched his face with the other. More memorable still was the solitary adventure of ringing, not for the first time, the bell of a big house and being run down by the coachman. As he was the son of our greengrocer, an agile middle-aged respectable woman with long curls, I expected him to behave leniently. But he shut me up in a dark outhouse for two hours. I took my revenge. The place contained sacks of oats for the horses, and into these I put a number of steel pens, having first broken them so as to make two sharp stiff points. These, I firmly hoped, would ultimately destroy the horses belonging to my tormentor's master. The hope gave me not only consolation, but a feeling of glory and power and evil as I at last hurried home to tea. [28]

And finally that spirit even had its literary hero; the boy's first important experience of books came with his reading of Richard Jefferies and the last words of *The Amateur Poacher*:

'Let us get out of these indoor narrow modern days, whose twelve hours somehow have become shortened, into the sunlight and the pure wind. A something that the ancients thought divine can be found and felt there still.' They were a gospel, an incantation. What I liked in the book was the free open-air life, the spice of illegality and daring, roguish characters – the opportunities so far exceeding my own, the gun, the great pond, the country home, the apparently endless leisure – the glorious moments that one could always recapture by opening the *Poacher* – and the tinge of sadness here and there as in the picture of the old moucher perishing in his sleep by the lime kiln, and the heron flying over in the morning indifferent. Obviously Jefferies had lived a very different boyhood from ours, yet one which we longed for and supposed ourselves fit for. [29]

The Amateur Poacher (1879) is exactly a celebration of the rural counter-culture, a real adult world which in fact is merely an extension of all the 'values' suggested in the world of *The Childhood*. Here is an ideal republic of layabouts and mouchers, of lurchers and rustic wide-boys; in Jefferies' own words:

The reason of these things is that Sarsen has no great landlord. There are fifty small proprietors, and not a single resident magistrate. Besides the small farmers, there are scores of cottage owners, every one of whom is perfectly independent. Nobody cares for anybody. It is a republic without even the semblance of a Government. It is liberty, equality, and swearing. As it is just within the limit of a borough, almost all the cottagers have votes, and are not to be trifled with. The proximity of horse-racing establishments adds to the general atmosphere of dissipation. Betting, card-playing, ferret-breeding and dog-fancying, poaching and politics, are the occupations of the populace. A little illicit badger-baiting is varied by a little vicar-baiting; the mass of the inhabitants are the reddest of Reds. Que voulez-vous? [30]

This is, of course, the recidivist imagination's Utopia. And now we can realise to what an extent there is in Edward Thomas's work, on one side, the over-powering desire to escape into this savage amoral masculine society. There are no serious women in this state. The desire to run away from a whole civilisation into a careless existence is very powerful in Western writing – we need think here only of Huckleberry Finn – but that should not obscure the fact that in Edward Thomas's case, at least, this is no comedy. The effects of this escapist dream on his life were disturbing and pathetic. When the sense of entrapment became too strong, when home made him sick, he would leave his family and go on endless tramps – back and forth across England, a haunted figure moving and usually fast across the landscape: obsessed by roads. On a piece of paper, found on his body, he had written the line 'Roads shining like river up hill after rain'.[31] And this is the fragment of the other; the power of the thought lies in its concentration of the images of streams (a recurrent metonymy) and roads – life leading anywhere, somewhere: away.

And yet we have failed to give the proper account if the matter rests there. For Edward Thomas was a poet and poetry has – evidently – to be accounted for in the child's development. If the escapist power of Jefferies' *Amateur Poacher* lies in an adolescent rejection of polite society, it is important to remember that the apparently bonding force of sexual desire may initially express an aggressive defiance of constriction, of laws and conventions. In Edward Thomas's case, sexual desire is alluded to at moments throughout *The Childhood* but always as an ache, as a light pressure building up beyond the clear edge of experience until, perforce, it begins to make its unavoidable claims, begins to demand its articulation. And this it does – naturally but ironically enough – through the discovery of poetry:

> So on Sunday when Jimmy and I walked out in our best clothes I took Tennyson with me. The fact that there might be a girl there whom I wanted to know did not enable me to stand much of the Sunday crowd, and very soon I turned aside and began to read Tennyson, sometimes aloud. Jimmy scoffed impatiently . . . I am almost certain that the reading of poetry was connected with my liking for a girl named Blanche. [32]

As Helen Thomas recalls it in *As It Was*: 'We were still very ignorant of sex, and only knew in a vague way through the reading of poetry how the human sexual act was performed. I remember very well with what joy I realised that his head would be on my breast, and I

would enfold him in my arms'.[33] He read poetry to her that day on
Clapham Common. So they learned soon enough. The poetry and
the sex – as we know – ironically transformed the freedom of their
youthful (childish?) physical self-expression into an imprisonment.
The time-span between the vanishing childhood and oppressive
adulthood is very brief. Too soon Edward Thomas's rebellious
selves – the 'poaching self', the 'poetic sexual self' – disappear
under the weight of other people's books and his own children.

The birth of the poet thus comes about from and through these
perplexing ironies. And the poetry is expressive of the very process
of its conception – as in 'Home' and 'The long small room' – while
seeking to get beyond the conflicting worlds which engender it.
And as it does so we move past them into another existence whose
beginning is more easily graspable than its end.

Edward Thomas began to write his first poems in late 1914; in
July of 1915 he enlisted in The Artists' Rifles and from then on
wrote prodigiously. This may be understood first by the fact
of Robert Frost's encouragement and second by the economic
liberation offered by service – he now had a patron, His Majesty
the King. And here we have to realise that the poetry was written
only during that period of training in England before being shipped
to the Front. In this sense Edward Thomas is not a War poet. This
is what makes the verse so increasingly strange, so haunting: it is
not, in origin, simply poetry of the home and family; nor is it, in
conclusion, poetry of the army; it is neither of the feminine world of
its past; nor of the escapist/masculine world of its future. He writes
as he waits for the war: the poetry increasingly a language of the
limbo, suspended amongst these lives. The soldier who can still go
home explores a new – distinct – state of mind: namely a chilling
indifference. Edward Thomas becomes in the end the poet of the
darkness which he awaits: the last line of his last poem contemplates
life 'Removed eternally from the sun's law'.[34]

This – then – is the poet of 'Rain' who thinks, as he lies alone, in
his hut listening to the storm, of these things:

> Rain, midnight rain, nothing but the wild rain
> On this bleak hut, and solitude, and me
> Remembering again that I shall die
> And neither hear the rain nor give it thanks
> For washing me cleaner than I have been
> Since I was born into this solitude.

Blessed are the dead that the rain rains upon:
But here I pray that none whom once I loved
Is dying tonight or lying still awake
Solitary, listening to the rain,
Either in pain or thus in sympathy
Helpless among the living and the dead,
Like a cold water among broken reeds,
Myriads of broken reeds all still and stiff,
Like me who have no love which this wild rain
Has not dissolved except the love of death,
If love it be towards what is perfect and
Cannot, the tempest tells me, disappoint. [35]

These are the lines of blank farewell. An empty present – the past is dead, the future death – awaits the return of the darkness out of which all has come. 'Waiting for the end, boys'[36] – as Empson sardonically put it about another poet: but Edward Thomas *was* the poet of the end, of the ends he had gone through; was going through.

Here love ends –
Despair, ambition ends;
All pleasure and all trouble,
Although most sweet or bitter,
Here ends, in sleep that is sweeter
Than tasks most noble.[37]

He had gone through the home, left it, to get through the poetry and now the poetry exists to signal the next journey, that which is beyond itself. These are the testaments of a dark voyage – complex postcards about nowhere sent to no one – progressing towards death.

Once he left England and arrived at the Front, at the War, there were no more poems. He kept a diary which records odd lines; but in effect the entries are observer's notes on men and animals: a naturalist of the War. For at the Front there was nothing left to write poetry about or for. Messing about in trenches won't stand for description but in a sense here was the final escape, the ultimate moucher society, the world of gibbets and evildoers, of poachers and villains. This time there were serious rats. And this time you too were the prey. So what was left? Here was no need for poetry; for all that struggle. The self was nailed up on a gate-post of the past. Now you could potter about with the chaps, write home, and unassumingly pretend to think cheerfully about things as you waited for the mine, the shell, the bullet. Here was the constant clear-light of the last minute before re-entering that sweet darkness beyond all pleasures, all pains of conflicting experience. Thus the last entry in his Diary: 'Neuville in early morning with its flat straight crest with trees and houses – the beauty of this silent empty scene of no inhabitants and hid troops, but don't know why I could have cried and didn't'.[38]

2

Toad Eating: Ivor Gurney

Look for Ivor Gurney in *The New Oxford Book of English Verse* and you will be disappointed. Look for him in Larkin's *Oxford Book of Twentieth Century English Verse* and you will find only this:

Strange Hells

There are strange Hells within the minds War made
Not so often, not so humiliatingly afraid
As one would have expected – the racket and fear guns made.
One Hell the Gloucester soldiers they quite put out;
Their first bombardment, when in combined black shout
Of fury, guns aligned, they ducked lower their heads
And sang with diaphragms fixed beyond all dreads,
That tin and stretched-wire tinkle, that blither of tune;
'Après la guerre fini' till Hell all had come down,
Twelve-inch, six-inch, and eighteen pounders hammering Hell's
    thunders.

Where are they now on State-doles, or showing shop patterns
Or walking town to town sore in borrowed tatterns
Or begged. Some civic routine one never learns.
The heart burns – but has to keep out of face how heart burns.[1]

This sonnet appeared in Blunden's 1954 edition of Gurney's verse and so seems a representative choice for that reason. Here was an example of Gurney's work from the first attempt to rehabilitate the poet after his death. Furthermore, it is a good anthology example because it gives the reader of *The Oxford Book* an immediate entry into Gurney's world. Here is the characteristic attention to form even if the sonnet is somewhat slovenly ('Bohemian') in rhyme and metre. But, then again, that nicely suggests how the nightmare of a strafe would probably suspend – at the very least – interest in neatly made verse while nonetheless asserting the very necessity of the rage – at all costs – for order. The whole bloody racket ('black shout') the poem remembers is transcended by the Gloucesters in song.

'That tin and stretched-wire tinkle, that blither of tunes' is an acute response to sound within sound – the fragile tinkle ironically bringing barbed-wire to mind – with the unexpected word 'blither' existing ironically between 'blather/blether' or 'blithering' ('senselessly talkative' *O.E.D.*) on the one hand and 'blithe/blither' ('exhibiting kindly feelings'; being 'joyous, glad') on the other. And the form actually is at work within this heightened sensitivity to sound, as the tenth line overruns any metrical constraint, charging on towards the *silence* of a sonnet turn –

Twelve-inch, six-inch and eighteen pounders hammering Hell's thunders.

– and the fact not of death and destruction but survival: the dreary wasted lives in a doleful postwar culture for which they are/have no use. Finally, beyond all that, the last line, with its strangely forceful economy, suggests a gnomic observation about anger and self-control – recalling thereby the very activity the poem has articulated. Or is it shame? The burning face disguised?

So far, then, it seems Larkin has chosen a poem worthy of inclusion: indeed is it not in the singularity of a whole group's experience – the Gloucesters – that we have exactly the qualities a solitary anthology piece should possess? It stands as witness, as an enlightening point, of historical reference. We learn what it was like to be there. But, then again, the very idea of 'representativeness' cripples the poem's claim to meaning. To value the work because of some documentary significance reveals the very conceptual problem of any traditional diachronic anthology. Historical and aesthetic judgements will diverge. Thus it becomes impossible to overcome the faint praise intrinsic to solitary existence: was that the *only* good poem Gurney wrote? No, but it's no worse than the rest. If not completely forgotten, the unfortunate poet is marginalized: whatever else is to be said from the evidence of a solitary sonnet there is no question here of centrality, of traditional significance. Which, of course, reminds us that important anthologies are the treacherous reality of Eliot's 'ideal order'.

There have been two *Oxford Books* of modern verse compiled by great poets: to have been ignored by Yeats at least put Gurney in very good company, but to have fared so ill at the hands of Larkin is remarkable. Perhaps the quarrel here is not with the specific cause of injustice but rather with the values of a whole literary culture: it should, quite simply, have been impossible to have composed a volume of twentieth century verse which could omit, for example, 'The Lock Keeper', 'War Books', 'The Silent One', 'The Dearness of Common Things', 'The Interview', 'Quiet Fireshine', 'Sonnet – September 1922', etc. etc.

But, then again, life is change: words move. In the same year Larkin's anthology was published, 1973, a new edition of Gurney's verse appeared with Blunden's introductory essay of 1954. Leonard Clark's selection must have had some effect; in 1978, Michael Hurd's remarkably moving biography appeared, and, in turn, *The Ordeal of Ivor Gurney* prepared the way for P. J. Kavanagh's currently definitive *Collected Poems of Ivor Gurney* in 1982. The following year a volume of *War Letters* was published and Geoffrey Hill delivered the F. W. Bateson Memorial Lecture on 'Gurney's Hobby'. This, then, is change. And yet, and yet: we have after all just passed the fiftieth anniversary of Gurney's death, an event which seems to have aroused little in the way of thanks for the poet and musician's work, if not life.[2]

'In making my selection I have striven to hold a balance between the different considerations that press on anyone undertaking a book of this kind. At first I thought I would let the century choose the poets while I chose the poems, but outside two or three dozen names this did not really work'.[3] Larkin's acknowledgement here, that theoretical problems are equally practical, helps us to accept the nature of his enterprise and express some kind of gratitude that at least Gurney got in – even if only to the margin. His editorial attention was, after all, focussed upon – among others – Hardy and Edward Thomas which, in a sense, reinforces the suspicion that decades of neglect needed revising. It may seem obvious now that Yeats was an eccentric man of straw in his *Oxford Book of Modern Verse* and that a selection of four poems by Hardy, one by Edward Thomas, none by Wilfred Owen or Robert Graves simply serves to confirm this; but then again consider the fact that *Scrutiny* was, throughout its entire run, oblivious to *Goodbye To All That*, *Undertones of War* and the *Sherston Memoirs*. Indeed Sassoon's verses – according to Leavis – might find 'in certain social *milieux*, their function'[4] and Graves's historical fiction – *Claudius the God* – could be considered by D. W. Harding as more fun perhaps than weekend gardening (indeed 'Even by more exacting standards you can at least read the whole book and retain your self-respect')[5] but that was it.[6] What lies behind this droll condescension; those turned blind eyes? Perhaps there was a Great War memoir strangled within Leavis's own soul? Or did he simply want to forget? Whatever, the only writer of 'War Books' worthy of serious consideration was Isaac Rosenberg and the reasons given by Harding for his exceptional centrality reveal the prejudices so deeply at play in the general rejection: '[T]here is in his work, without the least touch of coldness, nevertheless a certain impersonality: he tried to feel in the war a significance for life as such, rather than seeing only its convulsion of the human life he knew'.[7] The key word here is – of course – 'impersonality'. Further on in his brief account of Rosenberg's work, Harding tries to make the word carry the full weight of his intentions: 'In "Troopship" and "Louse Hunting" there is no civilian resentment at the conditions he writes of. Here as in all the war poems his suffering and discomfort are unusually *direct*; there is no secondary distress arising from the sense that these things *ought not* to be. He was given up to realizing fully what *was*.'[8] This is a liberating definition – at first sight: the 'impersonality' here seems to take us back to the first modern war poet, Whitman, and his promiscuous language's triumph over judgemental morality.

As I Lay with my Head in Your Lap Camerado

As I lay with my head in your lap camerado,
The confession I made I resume, what I said to you and the
    open air I resume,
I know I am restless and make others so,
I know my words are weapons full of danger, full of death,
For I confront peace, security, and all the settled laws, to
    unsettle them,
I am more resolute because all have denied me than I could
    ever have been had all accepted me,
I heed not and have never heeded either experience,
    cautions, majorities, nor ridicule,

And the threat of what is call'd hell is little or nothing to me,
And the lure of what is call'd heaven is little or nothing
    to me;
Dear camerado! I confess I have urged you onward with
    me, and still urge you, without the least idea what is our
    destination,
Or whether we shall be victorious, or utterly quell'd and
    defeated.[9]

But perhaps this is a deception. Ironically, the true shadow behind Harding's 'impersonal' Rosenberg is Eliot's 'individual talent'. The poet has no personality, has no self other than the creating focus of language:

> What happens is a continual surrender of himself as he is at the moment to something which is more valuable. The progress of an artist is a continual self-sacrifice, a continual extinction of personality.[10]

Rosenberg, Harding observes, had a willingness – and an ability – to let himself be new: 'not subduing his experience to his established personality.'[11]

And no doubt this is true of Rosenberg, but it still fails to create the conditions for an analysis of the following surreal passage by Blunden, for example: what is the 'personality' which should interest us here?

> The tunnellers who were so busy under the German line were men of stubborn determination, yet, by force of the unaccustomed, they hurried nervously along the trenches above ground to spend their long hours listening or mining. At one shaft they pumped air down with Brobdingnagian bellows. The squeaking noise may have given them away, or it may have been mere bad luck, when one morning a minenwerfer smashed this entrance and the men working there. One was carried out past me, collapsing like a sack of potatoes, spouting blood at twenty places. Cambrin was beginning to terrify. Not far away from that shafthead, a young and cheerful lance-corporal of ours was making some tea as I passed one warm afternoon. Wishing him a good tea, I went along three firebays; one shell dropped without

warning behind me; I saw its smoke faint out, and I thought all
was as lucky as it should be. Soon a cry from that place recalled
me; the shell had burst all wrong. Its butting impression was
black and stinking in the parados where three minutes ago the
lance-corporal's mess-tin was bubbling over a little flame. For
him, how could the gobbets of blackening flesh, the earth-wall
sotted with blood, with flesh, the eye under the duckboard, the
pulpy bone be the only answer? At this moment, while we looked
with intense fear at so strange a horror, the lance-corporal's
brother came round the traverse.

He was sent to company headquarters in a kind of catalepsy.
The bay had to be put right, and red-faced Sergeant Simmons,
having helped himself and me to a share of rum, biting hard
on his pipe, shovelled into the sandbag I held, not without self-
protecting profanity, and an air of 'it's a lie; we're a lie.'[12]

Blunden's prose ('the eye under the duckboard') seems to veer
both towards Harding's definition and then again deny it: 'we're a
lie' – or at least resolve itself into strange ambiguities; which 'we'
is the lie? Both?

II

Gurney's music, on the other hand, was subject to a *Scrutiny* review.
Perversely, given all this, Wilfred Mellers in 1938 judged that 'his
position in English music is somewhat similar to that of Edward
Thomas in English poetry, though [it is doubtful] if he has any
quality corresponding to Thomas's irony and delicacy of fibre':
whatever that may mean. 'Gurney's is a timid genius' a 'serious
composer, if a very little one.'[13] All of which may be true of Gurney
the composer (I am not competent to judge) but certainly would
be a travesty of Gurney the poet. As for the analogy with Edward
Thomas, let us put that to one side. Of course the residual irony
still points back to Larkin's problem which comes to him – and
us – through the struggle with those two or three dozen names,
the 'tradition', the centre, the ideal 'reality' of our culture. Mellers'
condescending comparison of Gurney to Edward Thomas is as
symptomatic pathologically as *Scrutiny*'s exclusion of major War
poets and major War prose. And therein lies the problem: 'War
Books'. The development of English poetry and the thinking of it

in this century has been perverted and distorted by the extremes
suggested through the label 'War Poetry'. It is this very distortion
which Larkin's anthology, in its limited way, begins to correct. So
that we should start from the acknowledgement that Larkin saw to
it that Gurney should, at least, get in and from there – the margins
of the *Oxford Book of Twentieth Century Verse* – see how far we
can reveal a centrality in the extreme conditions of Gurney's life
and art.

III

Helen Thomas remembers the day she first met Ivor Gurney:

> We arrived at Dartford Asylum which looked like – as indeed it
> was – a prison. A warder let us in after unlocking a door, and
> doors were opened and locked behind us as we were ushered
> into the building. We were walking along a bare corridor when
> we were met by a tall gaunt dishevelled man clad in pyjamas
> and dressing gown, to whom Miss Scott introduced me. He
> gazed with an intense stare into my face and took me silently
> by the hand. Then I gave him the flowers which he took with the
> same deeply moving intensity and silence. He then said, 'You are
> Helen, Edward's wife and Edward is dead.' And I said, 'Yes, let
> us talk of him.'
>   So we went into a little cell-like bedroom where the only
> furniture was a bed and a chair. The window was high and
> barred and the walls bare and drab. He put the flowers on the
> bed for there was no vessel to put them in; there was nothing in
> the room that could in any way be used to do damage with – no
> pottery or jars or pictures whose broken edge could be used as a
> weapon.
>   He remarked on my pretty hat, for it was summer and I had
> purposely put on my brightest clothes. The gay colours gave him
> great pleasure. I sat by him on the bed and we talked of Edward
> and of himself, but I cannot now remember the conversation. But
> I do remember that though his talk was generally quite sane and
> lucid, he said suddenly, 'It was wireless that killed Edward', and
> this idea of the danger of wireless and his fear of it constantly
> occurred in his talk. 'They are getting at me through wireless.'
> We spoke of country that he knew and which Edward knew too

and he evidently identified Edward with the English countryside, especially that of Gloucestershire.

I learned from the warder that Ivor Gurney refused to go into the grounds of the asylum. It was not his idea of the country at all – the fields, woods, water-meadows and foot-paths he loved so well – and he would have nothing to do with that travesty of something sacred to him.

Before we left he took us into a large room in which was a piano and on this he played to us and to the tragic circle of men who sat on hard benches built into the walls of the room. Hopeless and aimless faces gazed vacantly and restless hands fumbled or hung down lifelessly. They gave no sign or sound that they heard the music. The room was quite bare and there was not one beautiful thing for the patients to look at.

We left and I promised to come again.

Ivor Gurney longed more than anything else to go back to his native Gloucestershire, but this was not allowed for fear he should again try to take his own life. I said, 'But surely it would be more humane to let him go there even if it meant no more than one hour of happiness before he killed himself.' But the authorities could not look at it in that way.

The next time I went with Miss Scott I took with me Edward's own well-used ordnance maps of Gloucestershire where he had often walked. This proved to have been a sort of inspiration for Ivor Gurney at once spread them out on his bed and he and I spent the whole time I was there tracing with our fingers the lanes and byways and villages of which Ivor Gurney knew every step and over which Edward had also walked. He spent that hour in revisiting his home, in spotting a village or a track, a hill or a wood and seeing it all in his mind's eye, with flowers and trees, stiles and hedges, a mental vision sharper and more actual for his heightened intensity. He trod, in a way we who were sane could not emulate, the lanes and fields he knew and loved so well, his guide being his finger tracing the way on the map. It was most deeply moving, and I knew that I had hit on an idea that gave him more pleasure than anything else I could have thought of. For he had Edward as companion in this strange perambulation and he was utterly happy, without being over-excited.

This way of using my visits was repeated several times and I became for a while not a visitor from the outside world of war and wireless, but the element which brought Edward back to life for him and the country where they two could wander together.[14]

Here then the blind seeking to be led by the blind: the Edward Thomas we know, the man for whom life had been reduced to 'Not the end; but there's nothing more'; the drifter of inner space 'removed eternally from the sun's law', for whom the outer world, the world of Gurney's ordnance map fantasy, the fabled English earth, was merely a greater prison; the wanderer, in short, for whom existence had become servitude to his inferiors – this, for Gurney, was a profound source of consolation? Had he never read 'When first'?

When first

When first I came here I had hope,
Hope for I knew not what. Fast beat
My heart at sight of the tall slope
Of grass and yews, as if my feet

Only by scaling its steps of chalk
Would see something no other hill
Ever disclosed. And now I walk
Down it the last time. Never will

My heart beat so again at sight
Of any hill although as fair
And loftier. For infinite
The change, late unperceived, this year,

The twelfth, suddenly, shows me plain.
Hope now, – not health, nor cheerfulness,
Since they can come and go again,
As often one brief hour witnesses, –

Just hope has gone for ever. Perhaps
I may love other hills yet more
Than this: the future and the maps
Hide something I was waiting for.

One thing I know, that love with chance
And use and time and necessity

Will grow, and louder the heart's dance
At parting than at meeting be.[15]

But, of course, it may well be that a hopelessness seeking only
death in 'the future and the maps' ironically could reassure a man
imprisoned within memories of his own landscape. As Blunden
observed, '[t]he immense love of his country which Gurney's
experiences as a child and a youth implanted was to act almost
as a tyranny over his poetical character'.[16] Over the whole character,
we might add. Certainly something very deep within the man is
sounded by the example of Thomas. Blunden again (here quoting
a witness): "'With blazing eyes, he would pour forth an endless
stream of talk on the English country, or on English poetry from
Chapman to Edward Thomas, full of pithy and often violent, but
always acute and exciting criticism".'[17] This was from the period
of his incipient madness. The association of Gurney with Thomas
and the countryside and Englishness is both touching and from our
perspective misleading: the temptation to turn back from thought
and retreat into the escape suggested by Thomas's 'Words' has to
be resisted.

> Out of us all
> That make rhymes,
> Will you choose
> Sometimes –
> As the winds use
> A crack in a wall
> Or a drain,
> Their joy or their pain
> To whistle through –
> Choose me,
> You English words?
>
> I know you:
> You are light as dreams,
> Tough as oak,
> Precious as gold,
> As poppies and corn,
> Or an old cloak:
> Sweet as our birds
> To the ear,
> As the burnet rose

In the heat
Of Midsummer:
Strange as the races
Of dead and unborn:
Strange and sweet
Equally,
And familiar,
To the eye,
As the dearest faces
That a man knows,
And as lost homes are[18]

Too much sound of music in all that, for we know how Edward Thomas's relationship to the language had in truth worked itself out through a mare's nest of contradictions. Nonetheless, the contradiction of those contradictions in 'Words' is an expression of the liberation Edward Thomas spent his life desperately believing in, so the poem, perhaps, is better when read within the whole web of his failures and embittered ambitions. Yet if we cannot now read innocent of Eliot's mandarin pronouncements about the responsibilities to tradition – as an aside 'Tradition and the Individual Talent' could only have been written by a Eurocentric American aghast at the destruction of the Great War – we should not ignore the truth which 'Words' skims over: namely the relationship of word to environment. This is trite but also something which Eurocentric American geniuses led us away from remembering. When Blunden reports the testimony to Gurney's 'blazing eyes' and the pithy, often violent, talk about poetry and Edward Thomas, we should respect the emotion within the intellect and remember that it was precisely in so far as he could not walk the English soil of Gloucestershire, precisely in so far as he found the grounds of the asylum repugnant, precisely in so far as Edward Thomas would remind him of what it was meant to mean to be 'English', that he was made mad. Here is Edward Thomas idealizing all that:

A writer in *The Times* on patriotic poetry said a good thing lately: 'There may be pleasanter places; there is no *word* like home.' A man may have this feeling even in a far quarter of England. One man said to me that he felt it, that he felt England very strongly, one evening at Stogumber under the Quantocks. His train stopped at the station which was quite silent, and only an old old man got in, bent, gnarled, and gross, a Caliban; 'but somehow he fitted in with the darkness and the quietness and the smell of burning wood, and it was all something I loved being part of.' We feel it in war-time or coming from abroad, though we may be far from home: the whole land is suddenly home. Wordsworth felt it in the valley near Dover immediately after landing in August 1802, when he wrote the sonnet beginning:

Here on our native soil we breathe once more.
The cock that crows, the smoke that curls, that sound
Of bells; – those boys who in yon meadow-ground
In white-sleeved shirts are playing; and the roar
Of the waves breaking on the chalky shore; –
All, all are English. . . .[19]

But this is a fantastical, hallucinatory, fictitious England, hardly the wild uncompromising mental landscape of Edward Thomas's best writing. So, what are we witnessing when Helen Thomas recalls Gurney's fingers in their 'strange perambulation' with her dead husband's spirit? Like the lunatic, the dead poet had spent a life running away from home: both were intensely conscious of their exile. When Edward Thomas truthfully writes of 'home' surely it is in the knowledge of the first poem with that title:

Not the end: but there's nothing more.
Sweet Summer and Winter rude
I have loved, and friendship and love,
The crowd and solitude:

But I know them: I weary not;
But all that they mean I know.
I would go back again home
Now. Yet how should I go?

This is my grief. That land,
My home, I have never seen;
No traveller tells of it,
However far he has been.

And could I discover it,
I fear my happiness there,

Or my pain, might be dreams of return
Here, to these things that were.

Remembering ills, though slight
Yet irremediable,
Brings a worse, an impurer pang
Than remembering what was well.

No: I cannot go back,
And would not if I could.
Until blindness come, I must wait
And blink at what is not good.[20]

'This is my grief': but was it to that Ivor Gurney responded? Is that the imaginary journey he took as he pored over the maps? Vagabonding with the other man? Freedom here is a terrible solitude, a deadness of soul which seeks release only in the roads. One of Edward Thomas's poems which Gurney set to music was 'Lights Out'; the title, of course, took his mind back to the Gloucesters and the community of soldiers with whom he had briefly found happiness, but the poem itself takes us on the road to oblivion: the free limbs seek extinction.

I have come to the borders of sleep,
The unfathomable deep
Forest, where all must lose
Their way, however straight
Or winding, soon or late;
They can not choose.

Many a road and track
That since the dawn's first crack
Up to the forest brink
Deceived the travellers,
Suddenly now blurs,
And in they sink.

Here love ends –
Despair, ambition ends;
All pleasure and all trouble,
Although most sweet or bitter,

Here ends, in sleep that is sweeter
Than tasks most noble.[21]

The end of all: love, despair, ambition. To Edward Thomas, roads
were potent living creatures whose power was both literal and
symbolic.

> Much has been written of travel, far less of the road. Writers
> have treated the road as a passive means to an end, and
> honoured it most when it has been an obstacle; they leave
> the impression that a road is a connection between two points
> which only exists when the traveller is upon it. Though there is
> much travel in the Old Testament, 'the way' is used chiefly as
> a metaphor. 'Abram journeyed, going on still toward the south,'
> says the historian, who would have used the same words had
> the patriarch employed wings. Yet to a nomadic people the
> road was as important as anything upon it. The earliest roads
> wandered like rivers through the land, having, like rivers, one
> necessity, to keep in motion. We still say that a road 'goes' to
> London, as we 'go' ourselves. We point out a white snake on
> a green hill-side, and tell a man: 'That is going to Chichester.'
> At our inn we think when recollecting the day: 'That road must
> have gone to Strata Florida.' We could not attribute more life to
> them if we had moving roads with platforms on the side-walks.
> We may go or stay, but the road will go up over the mountains
> to Llandovery, and then up again over to Tregaron. It is a silent
> companion always ready for us, whether it is night or day, wet
> or fine, whether we are calm or desperate, well or sick. It is
> always going: it has never gone right away, and no man is too
> late.[22]

This is more like it: '. . . a silent companion always ready for us. . .'.
We know that on the road – whether towards the woods lovely,
dark and deep or simply away from 'home', rounding the corner of
solitude – the will of man is drawn (in the going of the road itself)
towards the other, that which denies all the past's determining,
defining, controlling relationships. Edward Thomas's roads were all
travelled before he went to France: Ivor Gurney's – as the title of his
first volume *Severn and Somme* acknowledged – were the routes to
and from other worlds beyond the dimensions suggested even by
'Lights Out'. At least that seems the only way to approach the last
stanza of Ivor Gurney's 'Roads – Those Roads'.

Roads are sometimes the true symbolical
Representations of movement in the fate of man.
One goes from Severn of tales and sees Wales
A wall against England as since time began.

Hawthorn and poplar call to mind the different people
That ruled and had shaping of this land at their periods.
One goes from the Abbey to the smaller steeples,
There made worthy, and by tithe-barns, and all by roads.

Daylight colours grey them, they are stained blue by the
      April
Skies on their pools and summer makes carpet of dust
Fit for the royal; autumn smothers all with colour
Blown clean away by the withering cruel winter's gust.

Roads are home-coming and a hope of desire reached,
(There is the orange window at the curve of the dark way),
Whether by winter white frozen or by summer bleached,
Roads are the right pride of man and his anxiety.[23]

The last word is eery in its precise evocation of that state which
presumably Gurney and millions of other men felt as they marched
away from home; the road that takes you back to the orange
window equally takes you away to the front: anxiety enough
for any man to be swinging towards – say – the Somme. Edward
Thomas can begin his poem 'Roads' with the simple assertion – 'I
love roads' – but nonetheless the poem winds on towards the
melancholy realization that as of 22 January, 1916 (the date of
composition)

> . . . all roads lead to France
> And heavy is the tread
> Of the living; . . .

Although the poem believes it can integrate the imagined experiences of the road to death:

> . . . but the dead
> returning lightly dance:

> Whatever the road bring
> To me or take from me,

They keep me company
With their pattering,

Crowding the solitude
Of the loops over the downs,
Hushing the roar of towns
And their brief multitude.[24]

– it is an expression of utter innocence. The pattering will soon
enough be drowned in other sounds of the final journey –

[January] 29 [1917] Up at 5. Very cold. Off at 6.30, men marching
in frosty dark to station singing 'Pack up your troubles in your
old kit bag'. The rotten song in the still dark brought one tear.[25]

All roads lead to France: anxiety; Hell. Even so the mind attempts
to resist by keeping to the old habits of observation: for this is the
end. The roads had taken him all the way to this:

[March] 30 Bright early, then rain. New zero line, planting
pickets. Arranging for material for new O.P. dugout – old one
fell in yesterday. Clear and bright and still from 6 p.m. on.
Air full of planes and sound of whistles against Hun planes.
Blackbirds singing and then chuckling as they go to roost. Two
shells falling near Agny Chateau scatter them. Letters from Helen
and Mother and parcels from Mother and Eleanor. Too late to bed
and had no sleep at all, for the firing, chiefly 60-pounders of our
own. Shakespeare's plays for 10 minutes before sleep.

31. Up at 5 worn out and wretched. 5.9s flopping on Achicourt
while I dressed. Up to Beaurains. There is a chalk-stone cellar
with a dripping Bosh dug-out far under and by the last layer
of stones is the lilac bush, rather short. Nearby a graveyard for
the 'tapferer franzos soldat' with crosses and Hun names. Blackbirds in the clear cold bright morning early in black Beaurains.
Sparrows in the elder of the hedge I observe through – a cherry
tree just this side of hedge makes projection in trench with its
roots. Beautiful clear evening everything dark and soft round
Neuville Vitasse, after the rainbow there and the last shower.
Night in lilac-bush cellar of stone like Berryfield. Letter to Helen.
Machine gun bullets snaking along – hissing like little wormy
serpents.[26]

On his body – on that piece of paper which had the line 'Roads shining like river up hill after rain' – were also the lines

Where any turn may lead to Heaven
Or any corner may hide Hell[27]

which are a strange reduction of the seventh stanza of 'Roads':

The next turn may reveal
Heaven: upon the crest
The close pine clump, at rest
And black, may Hell conceal.

Heaven – instant death? Hell – an arm? a leg? blindness? insanity? The ends of anxiety.

There are strange Hells within the minds War made
Not so often, not so humiliatingly afraid
As one would have expected – the racket and fear guns made.

IV

But Ivor Gurney survived:

Blighty

It seemed that it were well to kiss first earth
On landing, having traversed the narrow seas,
And grasp so little, tenderly, of this field of birth.
France having trodden and lain on, travelled bending the knees.
And having shed blood, known heart for her and last nerve freeze,
Proved body past heart, and soul past (so we thought) any worth.
For what so dear a thing as the first homecoming,
The seeing smoke pillar aloft from the home dwellings;
Sign of travel ended, lifted awhile the dooming
Sentence of exile; homecoming, right of tale-tellings?
But mud is on our fate after so long acquaintance,
We find of England the first gate without Romance;
Blue paved wharfs with dock-policemen and civic decency,
Trains and restrictions, order and politeness and directions,

Motion by black and white, guided ever about-ways
And staleness with petrol-dust distinguishing days.
A grim faced black-garbed mother efficient and busy
Set upon housework, worn-minded and fantasy-free,
A work-house matron, forgetting her old birth friend – the sea.[28]

He was a lucky man: a survivor – lucky blighter. Getting sent home, that was what they all prayed for; sang about; dreamed of. Blunden's prose has the atmosphere of that communion:

> [T]here was the evening when Harrison took all the old originals and some others to the divisional concert-party performing in the town. The barn roof ought indeed to have floated away in the paeans and warblings that rose from us, as the pierrots chirruped and gambolled there. In sweet music is such art – and never was music sweeter than the ragtime then obtaining, if appreciation indexes merit. 'Take me back to dear old Blighty' was too much for us – we roared inanely, and when a creditable cardboard train was jerked across the stage and the performers looking out of the windows sang their chorus, 'Birmingham, Leeds or Manchester,' the force of illusion could no further go. . . . 'On the day on which Peace is declared,' a neat little skit, and 'When you're a long, long way from home' will never cease to ring pathetically through the years between. All the performers had been over the top. Glum and droll clown, where can I now find your equal?[29]

Of course, the next trick was staying out. Or even more, wanting to stay out. For Sassoon – as for Graves – the release into the calm and peace of home was intolerable. For they had knowledge of what had been done unto them, not to mention what they themselves had been encouraged – putting it mildly – to do unto others:

> But the star turn in the schoolroom was a massive sandy-haired Highland Major whose subject was 'The Spirit of the Bayonet'. Though at that time undecorated, he was afterwards awarded the D.S.O. for lecturing. He took as his text a few leading points from the *Manual of Bayonet Training*.
> . . .
> He spoke with homicidal eloquence, keeping the game alive with genial and well-judged jokes. He had a Sergeant to assist him. The Sergeant, a tall sinewy machine, had been trained to such a pitch of frightfulness that at a moment's warning he could divest

himself of all semblance of humanity. With rifle and bayonet he illustrated the Major's ferocious aphorisms, including facial expression. When told to 'put on the killing face', he did so, combining it with an ultra-vindictive attitude. 'To instil fear into the opponent' was one of the Major's main maxims. Man, it seemed, had been created to jab the life out of Germans. To hear the Major talk, one might have thought that he did it himself every day before breakfast. His final words were: 'Remember that every Boche you fellows kill is a point scored to our side; every Boche you kill brings victory one minute nearer and shortens the war by one minute. Kill them! Kill them! There's only one good Boche, and that's a dead one!'[30]

Making men mad killers: that was the objective. The problem, of course, for homicidal Majors was that men are various in their natures. There were elite units, true, who excelled in the ferocity of their raids: '"God strike me pink, Dick, it would have done your eyes good to have seen young Sassoon in that bombing stunt"' – the Royal Welch Fusiliers.[31] On the other hand, there were units which practised a belief in live and let live. Life could be very ugly if they ran up against a unit of Mad Jack Sassoons.[32] It is important to remember, then, that the front was part of an overall kaleidoscope of anxieties; moving up and back from different hostile sectors meant confronting unknown new adversaries. The pattern of trench war was thus an odd combination of the static and the kinetic. And holding all this together were the homicidal Majors: fierce disciplinarians necessary to encourage the men, whatever their character, to yerk the opposition under the ribs. Each man was forced to nurture the maniac inside himself: to control and yet sustain the violent other was essential. And this fact is crucial to any understanding of the relationship between Gurney's art and his madness. In due course, he became a machine-gunner; that made him a specialist killer: it would seem. Tony Ashworth –

To sum up, then, it may be that in a general sense war both attracts and creates violent persons, but the process is more marked with weapon specialists than others. I have found that violent attitudes against the enemy are relatively rare in personal documents of trench fighters and these attitudes seemed even less frequent among soldiers with whom I have spoken – one only, a shell-shock victim, admitted to hating Germans in the

war. On the other hand, such sentiments certainly did exist
among infantrymen and specialists but probably more often
among the latter than the former. 'Speaking for my companions
and myself, I can categorically state that we were in no mood for
any joviality with Jerry . . . we hated his guts', bluntly asserted
a machine-gunner of the 12th division. 'We were bent on his
destruction at each and every opportunity for all the miseries
and privations which were our lot. Our greatest wish was to be
granted an enemy target worthy of our Vickers gun.' Such an
animus against the enemy is consistent with the relative violence
of the specialist situation, ethos and war experience. Some believe
that battle brutalizes all soldiers, but if so, it dehumanizes some
more than others and in patterned ways.[33]

The extreme representation of this descent is found in Frederic
Manning's novel *The Middle Parts of Fortune*: the moral centre of
the narrative, Bourne, has survived the total degradation of trench
experiences and yet still seems capable of existing apart, sustaining
the role of a 'normal man' until his experiences of the Somme finally
plunge him into obscenities he had previously transcended. Finally
he can articulate the 'normal' discourse:

'Kid! You're all right, kid?' he cried eagerly.
    He was all right. As Bourne lifted the limp body, the boy's
hat came off, showing half the back of his skull shattered where
the bullet had come through it; and a little blood welled out
on to Bourne's sleeve and the knee of his trousers. He was all
right; and Bourne let him settle to earth again, lifting himself
up almost indifferently, unable to realize what had happened,
filled with a kind of tenderness that ached in him, and yet
extraordinarily still, extraordinarily cold. He had to hurry, or
he would be alone in the fog. Again he heard some rifle-fire,
some bombing, and, stooping, he ran towards the sound, and
was by Minton's side again, when three men ran towards
them, holding their hands up and screaming; and he lifted
his rifle to his shoulder and fired; and the ache in him became
a consuming hate that filled him with exultant cruelty, and he
fired again, and again. The last man was closest to him, but
as drunk and staggering with terror. He had scarcely fallen,
when Bourne came up to him and saw that his head was
shattered, as he turned it over with his boot. Minton looked at

him with a curious anxiety, saw Bourne's teeth clenched and bared, the lips snarling back from them in exultation.

'Come on. Get into it,' Minton cried in his anxiety.

And Bourne struggled forward again, panting, and muttering in a suffocated voice.

'Kill the buggers! Kill the bloody fucking swine! Kill them!'

All the filth and ordure he had ever heard came from between his clenched teeth; but his speech was thick and difficult. In a scuffle immediately afterwards a Hun went for Minton, and Bourne got him with the bayonet, under the ribs near the liver, and then, unable to wrench the bayonet out again, pulled the trigger, and it came away easily enough.

'Kill the buggers!' he muttered thickly.

He ran against Sergeant Tozer in the trench.

'Steady, ol' son! Steady. 'ave you been 'it? You're all over blood.'

'They killed the kid,' said Bourne, speaking with sudden clearness, though his chest heaved enormously. 'They killed him. I'll kill every bugger I see.' [34]

If one survives this – remember – one has to cohabit with the other. And which then becomes the true self? And which the true other? Out of the line and back into the 'real' world one took memories, presumably, if not a whole, integrated, soul. The *reality* of the self had been created in these multiple relationships with other men and their experiences: Graves and Sassoon recount the feelings of guilt and unease – of alienation – when back in England away from their own kind. And Blunden, brooding on his 'exeat' from the Third Battle of Ypres after months of utterly hellish fighting, writes about 'the distasteful process of separation from the battalion' and how he 'felt as usual the injustice of my own temporary escape while others who had seen and suffered more went on in the mud and muck'.[35] Or again, Sassoon, in 'Sick Leave', a poem he wrote at Craiglockhart War Hospital, reiterates the guilt and torment of surviving:

When I'm asleep, dreaming and lulled and warm, –
They come, the homeless ones, the noiseless dead.
While the dim charging breakers of the storm
Bellow and drone and rumble overhead,
Out of the gloom they gather about my bed.
    They whisper to my heart; their thoughts are mine.

'Why are you here with all your watches ended?
From Ypres to Frise we sought you in the Line.'
In bitter safety I awake, unfriended;
And while the dawn begins with slashing rain
I think of the Battalion in the mud.
'When are you going out to them again?
Are they not still your brothers through our blood?'[36]

V

So Ivor Gurney with his 'Blighty' and all his arms and legs and
eyes was truly a lucky man. For in his poem there seems to be none
of the dark recrimination that torments Blunden and Sassoon. It
seems right to kiss the earth now that narrow sea has taken him
from the other world – of muck and mud:

France having trodden and lain on, travelling bending the knees.
And having shed blood, known heart for her and last nerve freeze,
Proved body past heart, and souls past (so we thought) any worth.

In the obscurity of these lines there seems to be a recognition of a self
which had gone beyond all constraints or values of understandable
proportions: body past heart; soul past worth. The numbness is
the consequence of reflecting upon one's fragmented French self –
'travelling bending the knees' suggests a burden, servitude, as if
being crippled or maimed merely by having to traverse this foreign
soil. So it were 'well to kiss first earth/On landing'. The poem would
then seem to be about recuperation. The transformation from a
numb, fragmented, abstracted language of repression creates a
necessary opposite to Manning's release through the primal scream
('Kill the buggers! Kill the bloody fucking swine! Kill them!') since
now Gurney seeks peace, the reassertion of culture and values, the
calm of ordinary familiar things:

For what so dear a thing as the first homecoming,
The seeing smoke pillar aloft from home dwellings;
Sign of travel ended, lifted awhile the dooming
Sentence of exile; homecoming, right of tale-tellings?

'Homecoming': to be back among your own; home from exile to

tell tales for which a gaping crowd in the pub falls silent. And so 'Blighty' seems to possess a calm confidence which removes it from Sassoon's guilty rest-cure. It's the solidity of drab England we assume to be here celebrated. For what Gurney felt at the front, and how he understood his condition, is made clear in his letters to Marion Scott, close London friend, advisor and ultimately literary executrix:

> You are right about the roughness of some of my work; there is no time to revise here, and if the first impulse will not carry the thing through, then what is written gets destroyed. One virtue I know little of – that is, patience; and my mind is Hamlet's a wavering self-distrustful one, though quick and powerful at its times. Will Peace bring me peace, though? . . .
>
> What I said about trying to get a soft job is absolutely sincerely meant. Two years in the ranks, almost 9 months in France, is quite enough for one who loathes the life as I. Who has better right? And who desires Glory less? But the chief reason is, that no man in the company would blame me, but only envy. And anyway, here I am still, though at present in a haven of peace as odd job man at the canteen, which suits me very well. Only, it is undignified to go to frantic lengths for such a job.

The letter – this is February 1917 – goes on with a draft of the sonnet 'Pain'.

Pain

Pain, pain continual; pain unending;
Hard even to the roughest, but to those
Hungry for beauty . . . Not the wisest knows,
Nor most pitiful-hearted, what the wending
Of one hour's way meant. Grey monotony lending
Weight to the grey skies, grey mud where goes
An army of grey bedrenched scarecrows in rows
Careless at last of cruellest Fate-sending.
Seeing the pitiful eyes of men foredone,
Or horses shot, too tired merely to stir,
Dying in shell-holes both, slain by the mud.
Men broken, shrieking even to hear a gun.

Till pain grinds down, or lethargy numbs her,
The amazed heart cries angrily out on God.[37]

The force of this sonnet (published in *Severn and Somme*, 1917) was
for Gurney himself its very 'blackness', its utter contradiction of
Rupert Brooke's 'Sonnets of 1914':

Blow, bugles, blow! They brought us, for our dearth,
        Holiness, lacked so long, and Love, and Pain.
Honour has come back, as a king, to earth,
And paid his subjects with a royal wage;
        And Nobleness walks in our ways again;
And we have come into our heritage.[38]

Given that, it seems strange Gurney's poem has not achieved
the notoriety of, say, Sassoon's 'Attack'. The confidence of its
righteous anger is wonderfully controlled: details of the scene
emerge from the monotony of repetitions – 'pain, pain, pain';
'grey, grey, grey' – which suddenly circumscribe and identify the
'bedrenched scarecrows in rows' who are furthermore embedded
in that monotony by the internal rhyme. And when we learn
of mortality's cause – 'Slain by the mud' – we are appalled.
Men are 'bed-[w]renched' and then thrown into the earth – the
shellholes – where with shot horses they are expended, ground
down by fatigue and fear and lethargy. Sassoon ends 'Attack' with
the violence of that same hideous landscape of 'mud and muck':

Lines of grey, muttering faces, masked with fear,
They leave their trenches, going over the top,
While time ticks blank and busy on their wrists,
And hope, with furtive eyes and grappling fists,
Flounders in mud. O Jesus, make it stop![39]

The famous last utterance has its force in the doubly felt – and
sincerely so – prayer and its own blasphemy. This is illuminating
because we experience the fear and the moral outrage up to
a point. But Gurney's last line in 'Pain' – 'The amazed heart
cries angrily out on God' – arguably derives more force in its
assumption that the bewildered moral indignation, the 'amaze-
ment', comes from an innocence that has been betrayed by the
very source of love and life: God himself. The anger at the very

treachery of creation – the horses dying in this human war – is powerfully concentrated in the preposition 'on': what would be the difference if, setting aside the obviously inferior possibilities of, say, 'to' or 'for' the line read 'angrily out at God'? Simply, perhaps, that 'on' suggests genuine blasphemy – the anger is contemptuous – God is below and the angered human cries out on him accusations and imprecations. The heart's anger seeks him out.[40]

This poem was written a few months before Gurney got his 'sick-leave' and managed to get home safe and kiss the earth. So 'Blighty', returning to that, would seem to be a response utterly unlike Sassoon's in, for example, 'Sick Leave'; indeed, in its way, to be rather childish in the pleasure of getting out – having tales to tell. But it doesn't continue thus at all:

> But mud is on our fate after so long acquaintance,
> We find of England the first gate without Romance;
> Blue paved wharfs with dock-policemen and civic decency,
> Trains and restrictions, order and politeness and directions,
> Motion by black and white, guided ever about-ways
> And staleness with petrol-dust distinguishing days.
> A grim faced black-garbed mother efficient and busy
> Set upon housework, worn-minded and fantasy-free,
> A work-house matron, forgetting her old birth friend – the sea.

Here is something impenetrable: yet what is the problem? Is it in the line 'but mud is on our fate after so long acquaintance'? That may seem to tell all, indeed to suggest – contrary to earlier expectations – that the poem is closer to Blunden and Sassoon than we might have thought. The mud is a sinister unexplored 'fact', because so evidently there as a symbol: a mark, a stigma. The soldiers wear their marks which can never be washed away. But instead of pursuing that line, Gurney returns to the theme of peace and the release from France, returns to the subject, after all, of the poem: *'England'*. That is to say, he, Gurney, the returned soldier with feelings is not of interest. The place – home – England, that is what he confronts and the collision is eery – 'the first gate without Romance'? The land which they sang and dreamed of has, as it were, no Arthurian stratum to the layers of its history; no, this England (an England we might recall Lawrence was on the point of *leaving*) is ambiguously decent and peaceful, orderly and drab, without Romance certainly, but *with* what?

Blue paved wharfs with dock-policemen and civic decency

The line is balanced round paranoid observations lurking within 'policemen' and 'decency'. You're back with the mud on you – be decent now. You're back but are you meant to be back? Are the policemen there just to check that you're not some windy bugger who's faking shell-shock or whatever? Because if you are then . . .

Trains and restrictions, order and politeness and directions

Again there is the same double-edge to the commerce of peace and civilization – trains and restrictions: order and directions. The revelation is of repression. There is no freedom now. This is the England of DORA – the Defence of the Realm Acts:

By New Year's Day 1917 most British people of democratic views had become dismayed by the Defence of the Realm Acts, which had generally torpedoed civil liberties and had substituted courts martial for much civil law. Any 'reports likely to cause disaffection or alarm' had become an offence. The police and military were given the power to search and inspect any premises at any time, to seize documents or 'anything' else which the military had reason 'to suspect' was being used, or might be used, for subversive purposes. Anyone could be arrested without a warrant. Suspects could be detained by the military police almost indefinitely, until they could be dealt with in the normal course of civil jurisdiction. Military boards could force anyone to live or not to live in a specified area. These and other regrettable regulations had reduced most citizens to a paranoid furtiveness. They tended to avoid strangers, to utter nothing critical, and to refrain from reading or listening to anything defeatist or anti-patriotic. In stereotyped phrases they backed the war effort.[41]

Here is confinement and contortion – the movement in the line

Motion by black and white, guided ever about-ways

is deliberately disorienting, vertiginous. Motion where? How? Black and white? Movement ever about ways? Coloured-less movement? The line is lapsing into sound – the music of the words – at the cost of sense. But the sense can be recalled instantly

> And staleness with petrol-dust distinguishing days

which sums that all up in its concise and sardonic way: 'Petrol-dust'. *This* is the earth to kiss? *This* earth is too decent for the Flanders mud? What is it that men have been going mad for? A country in which even woman (metonym for England?) is rendered unlovely and unloving:

> A grim faced black-garbed mother efficient and busy

The mother – presumably in black for her lost son(s) – carries on as usual: but for what?

> Set upon housework, worn-minded and fantasy-free

The mind-forged manacles have been hammered out. For what is she working? For what was he fighting? For whom? For her? For me? For this?

> A work-house matron, forgetting her old birth friend – the sea.

This is the truth of England and its women: the culture now fantasy-free – ironically thus anticipating the 'workhouse' and the doubleness of both poverty and drudgery; of endeavour and failure. The mother becomes the matron: uncreative, oblivious to her procreative sexuality – the sea.

The last word leaps away from the imprisonment of the rest of the poem, suggesting fluidity and escape. Certainly we want to look – as Gurney did – west to Manhattan, say, and Whitman, not to the Channel and France. Some things are better left unsaid. For once you are mended they'll send you back – across the 'narrow seas'. Perhaps then the poem's enigmatic ending is truthful to the unstated fears that cross below the asserted values. The implications

of the seas! And it is this very enigmatic quality which makes
Gurney so compelling. On one level we *seem* to know him. But on
another . . .

VI

Certainly it is just as well to set out the facts here: that Ivor Gurney
was born in Gloucester in 1890, the second of four children,
the child of a tailor – David – and an eccentric and increasingly
unstable mother – Florence (née Lugg); that he was discovered to
have musical talent by the local vicar the Rev. Alfred Cheesman;
that he transcended the inhibitions of the English class system by
winning a Scholarship to the Royal College of Music; that he met
there Marion Scott who was to become his literary executrix; that
there he studied with degrees of diligence (but nota bene with signs
of eccentric truancy particularly around 1913); that as soon as War
was declared he volunteered, was rejected but finally drafted, by
February 1915, into the 2nd/5th Gloucester Regiment; that he
served on the Somme from October to December 1917, thence to
St. Quentin where at Verman on April 6, he caught one in the
arm but not a 'Blighty'; that he was then transferred to Machine
Guns at the Arras front and had his first volume of verse accepted
(*Severn and Somme*); that, in August of the same year, he was pushed
north to Ypres where in September he was gassed and at last got a
'Blighty'; that he recovered in hospital near Edinburgh but, even
so, by the beginning of 1918 was showing signs of instability which
recurred throughout the next four years as he tried unsuccessfully
to start his musical career while supervising the publication of his
second volume of verse (*War's Embers*) and thus in September of
1922, after repeated suicide threats to the police and magistrates, he
was committed by his family to Barnwood House Asylum whence
he was removed in December 1922 to Stone House, Dartford, where
he spent the rest of his life: that is until 26 December 1937 when he
died. That is what we know.

VII

On the other hand, all that simply reminds us of what we don't
and can't, perhaps, *know* about a life. We think back and shudder

in relief that we didn't lose our limbs, our eyes, our senses and assume that the act of writing about experiences of the Somme or Ypres must fundamentally be an exorcism of self-recreation. To write suggests a profound degree of control which is its own moral triumph. How then can such a mind be mad? Mellers called Gurney's musical genius 'timid'; the word seems offensive in whatever context of masculine life; it bears not the remotest relation to the man who suffered and the mind which created the *poems*.

> War brings greater self-control – or breakdown. You also must have mastery of yourself, or perish. And whether the pain be of complaining nerves or of waiting on age long nights of cold and wet to pass, it is all the same, and the use of patience brings the same reward. There is even the same uncertainty with us two, for instance – the same aching thought; whether we shall get the chance to use the rewards of patience. Indeed there is no difference in our conditions, save that I have the right to wear two 'wounded' stripes, and you can only want to do something – anything, to justify yourself to yourself. There again we are equal; for War is simply a necessary but horrid nuisance, and my aim is work in art, not a medal or a ribbon. Another consideration. Supposing I did get a DCM, I know well that braver men than myself have died without, and how to wear a distinction without shame, that is so uncertain in the earning?
>
> Please do not accuse yourself of uselessness. At any rate not to me, who have so much to thank you for.
>
> Our positions are reversed, and I am trying to cheer *you* up for once, instead of writing interminable complaints to get wise consoling words.[42]

'Wise consoling words' –

The Escape

> I believe in the increasing of life: whatever
> Leads to the seeing of small trifles,
> Real, beautiful, is good; and an act never
> Is worthier than in freeing spirit that stifles

Under ingratitude's weight, nor is anything done
Wiselier than the moving or breaking to sight
Of a thing hidden under by custom – revealed,
Fulfilled, used (sound-fashioned) any way out to delight:
Trefoil – hedge sparrow – the stars on the edge at night.[43]

What is the exact quality of the voice here? 'I believe': quiet,
certain, secure: or is it angry – 'Freeing spirit that stifles / Under ingratitude's weight'? Serious certainly: yes but lacking all
self-consciousness – indeed for its time radically so. Therefore is
it quaint; naive? No, for the certainty comes not simply out of
beliefs, nor even out of the very idea of belief itself, but from
something deeper: the values intrinsic to language's *sounds*. The
subtle metamorphosis of the poem's abstractions – 'real; beautiful;
good; worthier; spirit; ingratitude' – into the observations of perceived reality

Trefoil – hedge sparrow – the stars on the edge at night

occurs through the finest of abstractions – 'wiselier'. The act of
wisdom is found in the revelation through language itself – '(sound-
fashioned)' – of abstractions gone dead

. . . breaking to sight
Of a thing hidden under by custom

Noise which has moral value; surely this defines poetry: '(sound-
fashioned)'.

Which was not the case with the sounds of the War. For, apart
from the hideous detail of destruction, of the disgusting state to
which human beings reduced themselves or were reduced, if there
was any particular aspect of experience which obsessed those who
endured the front, it was the noise. To get out of that to peace! 'The
machine guns are the most terrifying of sound, like an awful pack
of hellhounds at ones back',[44] Gurney wrote to Marion Scott in
June 1916, a month after he had arrived in France. By August he
had isolated his anxiety in another letter to her:

The fear of death in sickness is widely different from that in a strafe. The most of us do not fear death very much. Hardly at all, in fact. It is hearing the shells and mortars soaring down to wipe you out, and the spiteful gibbering of the machine guns which *may* get you that does the trick. . . . The shattering crash of heavy shrapnel. The belly-disturbing crunch of 5.9 Crumps and trench mortars. The shrill clatter of rifle grenades and the wail of nosecaps flying loose. Sometimes buzzing like huge great May flies, a most terrifying noise when the thing is anywhere near you.[45]

In *No Man's Land: Combat and Identity in World War 1*, Eric Leed stresses the dreadful significance of this experience. It was impossible for any man who had been at the front to explain to a civilian what it was like – and here we are facing the extreme isolation of language from experience – for there were no words capable of expressing the sounds of battle. Graves's inability to reintegrate when on leave was caused by this dislocation: 'You couldn't [explain]: you can't communicate noise, noise never stopped for one moment – ever'.[46] And Leed concludes: 'The conditions of neurosis were created not by the sight of exploding chemicals but by the deafening sound and vibration of the barrage, which defenders were required to suffer for hours, even days'.[47] Huddled in the trenches, unable to see (or risk being sniped to peer over the top) living *in* the earth, waiting – *listening* – for the shells, gauging where they might land, the trajectory, from their sound through the air, men came to be tyrannized by noise. The ear dominated the eye and the result of this continuous assault (you can plug but not shut your ears) upon the sense was a profound disorientation of millions of psyches:

For the vast majority of Europeans who fought in the war, noise meant nothing but chaos; it caused nothing but fear, stupefaction, and dull resignation. Precisely because there was no cultural convention to call forth an appropriate switch of the soldier's 'inner state' during the transition from order to noise during the war, the barrage most often effected a transition into neurosis, breakdown, or mental disorder. The last defense against the murderous and brutalizing realities of war lay in bleak irony, projection, fantasy, or the assumption of a neurotic symptom.[48]

In 'A Note on War Poetry', Eliot asks

Where is the point at which the merely individual
Explosion breaks

In the path of an action merely typical
To create the universal, originate a symbol
Out of the impact?[49]

But is this the right question? It is not a matter here of the relation
between individual and universal experience, but rather of experience which is universal to a separate group of individuals while
nonetheless hostile to language at fundamental levels of meaning.
How do we make significant sound '(sound-fashioned)' out of
meaningless noise; communicate that which, by its very nature,
language directs us away from: chaos, disorder, insignificance?
Thinking back to 'The Escape' one registers the curiosity of the
title because the *poem* itself descends into meaning. It reminds us
of, say, William Carlos Williams insisting on the awareness (in
'By the road to the contagious hospital') of how noise ('sound-
fashioned') – words – should see.

One by one objects are defined –
It quickens: clarity, outline of leaf [50]

Life in its particularity is life in discrete clarity

Of a thing hidden by custom – revealed.

Revelation. In a sense then the title's meaning is actually at odds,
as it were, with the poem itself, pointing back at a whole range
of experience *from which* the poem is escaping; in effect from 'War
Books' and the experiences of, for example, 'On Somme':

Suddenly into the still air burst thudding
And thudding, and cold fear possessed me all,
On the grey slopes there, where winter in sullen brooding
Hung between height and depth of the ugly fall
Of Heaven to earth; and the thudding was illness' own.
But still a hope I kept that were we there going over,
I in the line, I should not fail, but take recover

From others' courage, and not as coward be known.
No flame we saw, the noise and the dread alone
Was battle to us; men were enduring there such
And such things, in wire tangled, to shatters blown.

Courage kept, but ready to vanish at first touch.
Fear, but just held. Poets were luckier once
In the hot fray swallowed and some magnificence.[51]

Here Gurney is attempting the impossible: to find the words that recreate the experience of the noise; to get at the fear that threatens to dishonour him. If the poem is remarkable it is precisely so as the key word 'thudding' becomes essential to the moral concern – 'not as coward be known' – since it, the 'thudding', is internalized: 'was illness' own'. The dreadful noise of the shells

Suddenly into the still air burst thudding
And thudding

is of monstrous infernal fists raining down upon the men in their filthy lairs and is, of course, also the thudding of the terror-struck heart threatening to break the spirit of courage Gurney seeks in fellowship. Hence the insistent first person pronoun

I in the line, I should not fail, but take recover

obviously seeks its sublimation within communality – 'no flame we saw' – in order to escape isolation and hence identification: 'as coward be known'. The truths of this transformation may be found in the odd phrase 'take recover' which, presumably, may be read as, on the one hand, to take 'cover' (hide) or, on the other, 'to recover' (recuperate; regain self-control) thus neatly suggesting cowardice and its opposite simultaneously. Yet there is a registered use of 'recover' as a noun, namely as the withdrawal of a thrust bayonet.[52] So the desired resolution of this conflict – to be transformed into a killer as demanded – is ironically hidden, covered, by our 'ordinary' use of words even as the mind anticipates a final terrible assault upon the ear:

No flame we saw, the noise and the dread alone

Was battle to us; men were enduring there such
And such things, in wire tangled, to shatters blown.

For, out 'there' – in No Man's Land – having gone over, are men
in the fire, the 'flame', being shredded into worthless dead flesh,
tangled and shattered: enduring 'such things'. The disgust in the
objectifications suggested by 'things' is, then, the moral indignation the poem seeks to communicate. Except, of course, it is a
sonnet and Gurney creates – with the separateness of the last
three lines – a turn. And the turn is expressive of the fear of
fear: 'Fear, but just held' – and those poor buggers out there in
the flame. Now the poet soldier lives in dread; humiliated by the
terror of thudding death – *hearing* destruction and recognizing that
there is nothing glorious, nothing noble, about all this – lacking all
'magnificence'.

This, then, is the world of experience 'The Escape' so calmly
refuses to allow back into the mind. But we know that the poem is
the result of a terrible struggle. That struggle is against the sounds
of madness:

Poem

Horror follows horror within me
There is a chill fear
Of the storm that does deafen and din me
And rage horribly near.

What black things had the human
Race in store, what mind could view?
Good guard the hour that is coming,
Mankind safe, honour bring through.[53]

It is the strength of Gurney's convictions which jolts us again and
again in his poetry. As the '(sound-fashioned)' (taking the double
sense of 'sound') art controls the sense of right and wrong, draws
upon emotions to find inspiration for expression, fashions then a
whole created response to and judgement about experience, we are
confronted by an honesty which offers no suggestion of timidity.
It is that honesty which is utterly admirable in Gurney's poetry:
unfortunately it may well be that same honesty which tragically

led him to deem his own life to be worthless. Nonetheless the honesty of his art is courageous: it insists upon the possibility of value in life – that the experiencing self can transcend its suffering, overcome the pain of noise and rediscover what must be good.

Midnight

There is no sound within the cottage now,
But my pen and the sound of long rain
Heavy and musical, I must think again
To find so sweet a noise, and cannot anyhow.

The soothingness and deep-toned tinkle, soft
Happenings of night, in pain there's nothing better
Save tobacco, or long most-looked-for letter . . .
The different roof-sounds – house, shed, loft and scullery.[54]

The belief in life focusses upon the details of existence: small sounds replace the monstrous din of battle. We forget – as pain indeed reminds us – what we take for granted; the beauty of 'roof-sounds' carries a range of associations: comfort, safety, calm, peace, health. The world reassures and offers what cannot be found within the self. But this struggle with dejection is continuous; the poems are part of a process – to survive survival. The fear of madness lurks within the work even as it asserts belief:

Quiet Fireshine

Quiet is fireshine when the light is gone,
The kettle's steam is comfort and the low song.
Now all the day's business stills down and is done
To watch them seems but right; nothing at all is wrong.

Save the dark thoughts within most bitter with
Disappointment, mere pain; gnawing at heart's peace.
The heavy heart so ponderous once was lithe
Travelling the hill slope easy at light's pace.

Quiet is fireshine, and the mind would soak
Years ago, after football, in drowse of light.

Now the slack body is sick and a bitter joke
To a soul too sick for dreams at fall of night.[55]

The concentration of meaning which is peculiar to Gurney's style – 'Quiet is fireshine' – reflects the intensity of concentration he brings to life. The seriousness of attention to living thus creates the threat of an excess of intellectual pressure: the dark is menacing and the synthesis of valued sounds with – evidently – spiritual and emotional light, offers us the edge of confession over self-pity. Light and lightness; the sound of fire 'speaking' quietly at night: at moments Gurney seems to confront Coleridgian dejection at a depth which is equal to the truths of Romantic art; for example:

Friendly Are Meadows

Friendly are meadows when the sun's gone in
And no bright colour spoils the broad green of grey,
And one's eyes rest looking to far Cotswold away
Under cloud ceilings whorled and most largely fashioned
With seventeenth-century curves of the tombstone way.
A day of softnesses, of comfort of no din, not passioned.
Sorrel makes rusty rest for the eyes, and the worn path,
Brave elms, and stiles, willows by dyked deep water-run –
North French general look, and a sort of bath
Of freshness – a light wrap of comfortableness
Over one's being, a sense as of music begun;
A slow gradual symphony of worthiness, fulfilledness.
But this is Cotswold, Severn: when these go stale
Then the all-universal and wide decree shall fail
Of world's binding, and earth's dust apart be loosed,
And man's worship of all grey comforts be abused,
To mere wonder at lightning and torrentous strong flying hail.[56]

There is a Wordsworthian majesty at the centre of this –

A slow gradual symphony of worthiness, fulfilledness.

– a recreation of a way to value the world which seemingly had vanished with the torments of the World War. In *The Waste Land*, Eliot could only appeal to foreign language and foreign soil to suggest a possibility of necessary relations between natural sounds and human meaning: 'What the Thunder said' is addressed, after all, to the jungles of Eliot's imagined academic Sanskrit world.

Here we can assent to assertions about the restorative powers of a familiar landscape even as we notice the qualifications: 'broad green of grey' may run with 'tombstone way', yet that only serves to naturalize the natural. Death is sensed as inevitably about in the land and sky but only as it always has – 'seventeenth century curves' – and always will be. And in the transformation of England to 'North French general look' we recognize a restoration; the balanced memory playing with the senses harmonizes differences so the very calm of the slight observation assumes a much greater victory than is explicitly stated. Yet nothing can anticipate the rapid disintegration the poem immediately experiences through that very metamorphosis: 'But this is Cotswold, Severn. . .' The reconciliation is immediately undone: this is not and cannot be Northern France exactly because a whole of values and beliefs – that this is certainly not the catastrophic landscape of Ypres and the Somme – is embedded in this physical material reality: here. And the weight of that opposition – there is no middle ground; no synthesis – is profound. If *this* loses its power, if *this* land becomes waste – 'earth's dust apart be loosed' – 'stale', then everything will fall apart. But we must remind ourselves that an extraordinary emphasis has been placed upon the minimality of experience: it is a 'grey' world at dusk and the moral value it suggests is largely in absences, particularly the softness 'of comfort of no din'. It is the poet's madness to lose that capability, for then alienation from life paradoxically turns round powerful presences:

. . . wonder at lightning and torrentous strong flying hail.

'Torrentous' is not in the *O.E.D.*: presumably it is Gurney's invention. Torrent is clear enough; perhaps it then has grafted upon itself the last syllable of adjectives like 'stupendous; tremendous; horrendous' or 'thunderous' or all. Reading back, the word that now becomes curiously unstable is 'wonder'. If we think of wonder

and its Christian connotations – 'Through mighty signs and won-
ders' (Paul: *Romans* 15; 19); 'No wonder of it. . .' (Hopkins: 'The
Windhover') – then indeed it might seem perverse to yield up
one's belief in the marvellousness of existence: its 'strong flying
hail'. On the other hand, the distorted natural world, turning
itself at the poem's end into those other landscapes, and their
ceaseless din, *that* is the perversion of all value. Indeed, the line
actually continues from its predecessor and has to be read in that
context:

> And man's *worship* of all grey comforts be abused,
> To *mere wonder* at lightning . . .

Here then the word 'wonder' may carry – through its qualify-
ing adjective – the sense of simply being curious about, specu-
lative of; noticing, but hardly with the force of awe: 'I wonder'. Significantly the word 'worship' thus focusses our attention upon, reminds us of, what has been valued earlier in the
poem – namely 'grey comforts'. So that the plea is for the unex-
ceptional, for the 'normal'. Merely to wonder at human lightning
and torrentous hail and/or even to be in awe of natural violence
is of less moral value than to worship the drab and colour-
less scene suggested by friendly, dusky meadows. If that be
lost, the belief in – effectively – calm monotony, then what comes
next?

> We Poets in our youth begin in gladness;
> But thereof come in the end despondency
>   and madness.[57]

Fire and noise: these seem – even as the line suggests energy and
force – the antithesis of life. But can that possibly hold? Is it not a
kind of hopeless escape? On June 19th, 1918 he wrote to Marion
Scott: 'This is a good-bye letter, and written because I am afraid
of slipping down and becoming a mere wreck – and I know you
would rather know me dead than mad, and my only regret is that
my Father will lose my allotment'.[58] But he couldn't go through
with it. And thus began the central tragic struggle of his life: the
war against himself and his culture.

VIII

In September 1922 he was committed to Barnwood House, in
Gloucester, a private asylum for the insane. In December he was
moved to the City of London Mental Hospital at Dartford, Kent. He
never saw Gloucestershire again.

> I who was a worker at dawn, who saw winter dawns even
> Walking from work, am stiffening, waiting in one
> Packed ward, where ceiling flat-white is for heaven,
> Electric-lamp bulbs for the night lights or great bright sun.
> If it were ever necessary or right to punish
> Me, why not labouring free in the open air –
> Or using for eighteen hours power that so diminish
> By not using . . .
> . . .
>   (from 'Memory')

The behaviour which led his family to take the step in 1922 was
described to me in conversation by his sister-in-law, Mrs Ronald
Gurney. 'He started going to the Police Station every morning
asking for a revolver because he wanted to shoot himself. In
the end the police came and said we'd have to do something
about him – and by that time it was either him or us – so we
got a doctor and a magistrate here and when they came Ivor was
as right as rain. They said, 'We can't commit this man. There's
nothing wrong with him.' So Pop [Ronald Gurney] said, 'You
go into the next room, pretend to read the newspaper, and see
what happens.' They did this, and sure enough, within a few
seconds, Ivor had crept up to one of them and said, 'I say, old
sport. You don't happen to have a revolver on you, do you?
I want to shoot myself.' – and that was that. They put him in
Barnwood.'[59]

Does not this story support P. J. Kavanagh's judgement that there
was 'something formidable about Gurney'?[60] For what strikes home
here is the bizarre image created – as Kavanagh further notes – of
self-control: 'old sport' calmly transforms the whole 'tone' of this
grotesque incident. The forces of authority are sent-up through
assumptions about language and class. 'Old sport': this makes nonsense of the power which Gurney is supposedly acknowledging

in his request – *you* chaps carry guns, don't you? But then Gurney carried a machine gun during the war, so there is the deeper ridicule of authority and power which the 'old sport' reminds us of. Going on a shoot? 'Old sport'?

This was a dangerous, tragic, game and we can accept that as the climax to four years of dreadful turmoil (the lost battle with paranoid delusions, noise, voices in his head; bombarded, as he believed Edward Thomas had been, by radio waves),[61] the final solution his family accepted must have seemed 'reasonable' to all points of view. Yet from our safe perspective (and Helen Thomas's '". . .[S]urely it would be more humane to let him go even if it meant no more than one hour of happiness before he killed himself." But the authorities could not look at it that way') it must appear a dreadful decision. The subversive wit of Gurney's eccentricity could not now retrieve his life from the resolute inflexibility of 'authority'.

He left Longford and, without invitation, moved in with his brother and sister-in-law, Ronald and Ethel Gurney, who lived in Worcester Street, Gloucester. By 1922 Ivor's behaviour and eccentricity had grown intolerable to his family. He was certified insane and committed to Barnwood House, a mental hospital near Gloucester. However, he escaped from there, cutting his hands badly on broken glass in the process. It was decided that he should be committed to an asylum a long way from Gloucester and from which he could not escape. On 21 December 1922 he was taken to the City of London Mental Hospital at Dartford, Kent, there to remain for fifteen years until his death on 26 December 1937.[62]

If the tragic truth of Gurney's life is that he was to be ever at war, it was a conflict with an entanglement of fronts. Battles with his family, battles with his self – these are clear enough and, as we know, surely the lot of most human kind; but when you cross a certain line and begin to take on – as Helen Thomas put it – 'the authorities', then paranoia confronts reality. The unease which runs beneath the calm of 'Blighty' – policemen at the dock; directions – is one aspect of a perception of the world which became increasingly bitter about the power particular groups within particular structures hold over individuals. And, of course, no experience of that could have been more brutally uncompromising than in the British Army.

IX

I tell you what, mamselle; when I return to England I am going to lie in wait for all men who have been officers, and very craftily question them on several subjects, and if the answers to my questions do not satisfy me, they may look out for squalls. This is deadly serious. Talk of the need of 'dithipline' wont suit me:

Yours very sincerely   Ivor Gurney[63]

It is not just that 'dithipline' might be an unpleasant but necessary fact of life, it was also clearly perceived by the private soldier – Gurney unlike Graves, Sassoon, Blunden or Edward Thomas was always that, one of the men – as an extension of English society's power structure. Frank Richards, whose reminiscences in *Old Soldiers Never Die* are a demotic classic of a private's War, offers in this anecdote a summary of the contempt the men had for that class of officers who knew little of the Front:

It was a glorious summer morning the next day and anyone who had visited this part of the Front would have thought it was the most peaceful spot in France. No shells coming over, no reports of rifles, and the larks were up singing beautifully. It was generally like this after a show. A Staff Colonel from the Corps visited the front line to see the crater, and a few old soldiers put the dead German officer on a fire-step, fixing a lighted candle in one of his hands and a small pocket Bible in the other. Just as the Staff officer approached them they fixed a lighted cigarette in his mouth. The Staff officer didn't stay long in that part of the trench. This was done out of no disrespect to the dead German officer, but just to give the Staff officer a shock; who I don't expect would have come up to the front line if the enemy had been shelling it. We all hated the sight of Staff officers and the only damned thing the majority seemed to be any good at was to check men who were out of action for not saluting them properly.[64]

It was not simply power which created resentment and then resentment's only safe response – subversive wit – but its encodement within a mass of regulations which paradoxically lent an apparently arbitrary quality to its execution. Blunden recalls marching back from the front at Thiepval as the Somme conflict continued into winter, elated at survival until he witnessed the exactitude of 'dithipline':

> So inexpressible was the exaltation of that day, and the solid ground was ethereal, not much being uttered from man to man for many miles. An old friend of ours, however, did not feel this. In his grimmer mood and best red tabs he rode up, shrilly calling me out of my planetary dream to him, and ordered me to arrest the transport sergeant for the offence of allowing what he called 'super-structures' on his vehicles. Poor Sergeant Luck on his black horse came up in confusion, accepted his fate and observations on his gross unmilitary character, and the General reluctantly went devouring elsewhere. The super-structures ('surely you can see them, Blunden? Why did you not immediately place this non- commissioned officer under arrest?') consisted chiefly of the illegal extra blankets which the batmen had contrived to collect for their winter campaign; and once again one innocent suffered while many guilty went free. I condoled with Luck, and he with tears in his eyes thought of his hitherto spotless name in the world of limbers and Maltese carts and horse-lines.[65]

Graves, in command of a detachment of Special Reservists in 1915, experienced the multitude of disciplinary offenses that could come through the Battalion Orderly Room for 'crime' ranging from desertion; using obscene language to a non-commissioned officer; being drunk and disorderly; 'committing a nuisance on the barrack room square . . . [i.e.] committing excreta'; to – (this admittedly unusual) – prostituting '"the Royal Goat, being the gift of His Majesty, the Colonel-in-Chief, from His Royal Herd at Windsor, by offering its stud-services for a fee to —, Esq., farmer and goat breeder, of Wrexham."'[66] And if the variety of regulations was clearly there to generate a variety of offences, the further variety of punishments could certainly accommodate the need to encourage the others. Graves's servant, Private ('Tottie') Fahy, on return from leave, having fallen in with one Sergeant Dickens, an old boozing chum from India days, joyfully celebrated the reunion:

> The next morning I was surprised and annoyed to find my buttons unpolished and only cold water for shaving; it made me late for breakfast. I could get no news of Tottie, but on my way to rifle inspection at nine o'clock at the company billet, noticed Field Punishment No. 1 being carried out in a corner of the farmyard. Tottie had just been awarded twenty-eight days of it for 'drunkenness in the field', and stood spread-eagled to the wheel of a company limber, tied by the ankles and wrists in the form of an X. He was obliged to stay in this position – 'Crucifixion' they called it – for several hours every day so long as the battalion remained in billets, and then again after the next spell of trenches. I shall never forget the look that my quiet, respectful, devoted Tottie gave me. He wanted to tell me that he regretted having let me down, and his immediate reaction was an attempt to salute. I could see him vainly trying to lift his hand to his forehead, and bring his heels together. The battalion police-sergeant, a fierce-looking man, had just finished knotting him up when I arrived. I told Tottie, for what that might be worth, that I was sorry to see him in trouble.[67]

And, of course, over and above 'Crucifixion' was the ultimate penalty: '"to suffer death by being shot"'. [68]

So when we think of Gurney and his response to the 'authorities' we should begin from the experience of military discipline. In his letters to Marion Scott he makes it quite clear that he was anything but an example of best spit-and-polish: '"A Good man, sir, quite all right. Quite a good man, Sir, but he's a musician, and doesn't seem to be able to get himself clean"':[69] the R.S.M. to the inspecting Colonel. And so it was possible to boast of being among 'The Bohemians' at camp –

> Certain people would not clean their buttons,
> Nor polish buckles after latest fashions,
> Preferred their hair long, putties comfortable,
> Barely escaping hanging, indeed hardly able;
> In Bridge and smoking without army cautions
> Spending hours that sped like evil for quickness,

(While others burnished brasses, earned promotions).
These were those ones who jested in the trench,
While others argued of army ways, and wrenched
What little soul they had still further from shape,
And died off one by one, or became officers.
Without the first of dream, the ghost of notions
Of ever becoming soldiers, or smart and neat,
Surprised as ever to find the army capable
Of sounding 'Lights out' to break a game of Bridge,
As to fear candles would set a barn alight:
In Artois or Picardy they lie – free of useless fashions.[70]

The fourth line is – obviously – there to check us: to transgress in
the context of this culture, the army, is to risk life? Fashion can
lead to punishment – even death? But surely this is extravagant
even for the British Army. The problem lies in the word 'hanging'. 'To suffer death by being shot' was the army way. For
example

> . . . a young officer sentenced to death for cowardice (there were
> quite a number of lads like that). He was blind-folded by a
> gas-mask fixed on the wrong way round, and pinioned, and
> tied to a post. The firing-party lost their nerve and their shots
> were wild. The boy was only wounded, and screamed in his
> mask, and the A.P.M. had to shoot him twice with his revolver
> before he died. [71]

So 'hanging' seems to cut across our assumed expectations; indeed
if it were to have a preconceived place within the possible range
of terminations it would surely be exactly in the first line of 'The
Silent One'

> Who died on the wires, and hung there, one of two –

But clearly the context of 'hanging' here is not as on the wires.
If we accept its normal sense then we must assume Gurney
has transferred his consciousness to civilian life, or rather, has
imposed civilian punishments for military transgressions – but to
what end?

In Bridge and smoking without army cautions
Spending hours that sped like evil for quickness
(While others burnished brasses, earned promotions).
These were the ones who jested in the trench.
While others argued of army ways, and wrenched
What little soul they had still further from shape,
And died off one by one, or became officers.

The confusion implicit in 'hanging' seems to resolve itself in the contrast of styles – the (civilian) Bohemians seem heroic in their refusal to acknowledge army ways: long haired, unkempt, *m'en foutistes*; an indication of something magnificent in their response to hideous reality

These were the ones who jested in the trenches

anticipating – and in the extreme – Yeats's men that come 'from the fortieth winter'

Proud, open-eyed and laughing to the tomb.[72]

That all works, but only in so far as it ignores the poem's sinister dialectic. If this were ordinary life, readers of *poems* might be assumed by the author to feel – all things considered – automatically on *this* side – the 'Bohemian' – rather than that – 'brass burnishers'. Or perhaps might not. But at least a clear division would be established. Having found its audience, the poem can present its conflict of values. What is wrong, after all, with earning promotion? What's right about long dirty hair? Except that the real conflict about style and culture, jests and arguments, is in fact ruthlessly dismissed. If you seek promotion then you are looking to increase the chance of death. The ratio of mortality, officers to men, was as follows:

	% of officers killed	% of other ranks killed
October 1914-September 1915	14.2	5.8
October 1915-September 1916	8.0	4.9
October 1916-September 1917	8.5	4.7
October 1917-September 1918	6.9	4.0

	% of officers wounded	% of other ranks wounded
October 1914-September 1915	24.4	17.4
October 1916-September 1916	17.4	14.0
October 1916-September 1917	17.6	12.3
October 1917-September 1918	17.1	13.9

[SOURCE: J. M. Winter, 'Britain's "Lost Generation" of the First World War', *Population Studies*, vol. 31, no. 3, November 1977; quoted in Trevor Wilson, *The Myriad Faces of War: Britain and the Great War, 1914–18*, p. 759]

So the pursuit of 'army ways' brought you, in effect, closer to mortality. At the the Somme the Germans carefully sniped out the officers as they led their men over the top. Better to drop-out, no? Which then brings a completely different set of moral conflicts to the front – namely that between heroism and cowardice. The 'Bohemian' risks death by asserting civilian indifference to army ways: the upholder risks death by becoming more prominent within the line of fire. But then again, the Bohemians risk death by their very carelessness –

and smoking without army cautions.

– surprised that a game of Bridge should be broken up, as that 'candles would set a barn alight'. Saki's last words in a shallow crater at Beaumont Hamel on 14 November 1916 : 'Put that bloody cigarette out'[73] – caution, common sense; fear rather – tragically articulate the qualities called for. Better those than a bullet through the head. A synthesized normality of conduct, something which draws upon the casual anarchic indifference of the Bohemians while equally respecting the communality of existence – responsibility, courage, order – cannot be registered by the poem because, in the end, either way

In Artois or Picardy they lie – free of useless fashions.

The registration of futility here is bleak indeed. That values are distorted by the war is inescapable. That Gurney despised 'dithipline' is clear. But equally he was a *soldier* living a precarious existence ('The life expectancy of a machine-gunner in battle on the Western Front has been computed at thirty minutes'[74]) so that the creation within the poem of a spiritual No Man's Land is chilling. Perhaps the truth lies in the line

Spending hours that sped like evil for quickness

with its evident play upon 'quickness'. For the waste of life in the hours speeding uncreatively past – 'In Bridge and smoking' – denies the very etymological strength of 'quickness'. The world is speeding up in its torrents of noisy hopeless futility. Drop it then – give it up. But you can't get out. Or can you?

The Silent One

Who died on the wires, and hung there, one of two –
Who for his hours of life had chattered through
Infinite lovely chatter of Bucks accent:
Yet faced unbroken wires; stepped over, and went
A noble fool, faithful to his stripes – and ended.
But I weak, hungry, and willing only for the chance
Of line – to fight in the line, lay down under unbroken
Wires, and saw the flashes and kept unshaken,
Till the politest voice – a finicking accent, said:
'Do you think you might crawl through there: there's a hole.'
Darkness, shot at: I smiled, as politely replied –
'I'm afraid not, Sir.' There was no hole no way to be seen
Nothing but chance of death, after tearing of clothes.
Kept flat, and watched the darkness, hearing bullets whizzing –
And thought of music – and swore deep heart's deep oaths
(Polite to God) and retreated and came on again,
And retreated – and a second time faced the screen.[75]

Geoffrey Hill puts us onto the central episode here:

The perfect good manners . . . are simultaneously a tone-poem of the class-system, and a parody of what it is that brings two men, through the exercise of traditional discipline and reason, into a situation of unpremeditated terror and absurdity. [76]

Hill observes how, within the absurdity of this conversation there is an anticipation of the tragic realization that '[t]he "finicking accent" is the voice that calls the tune'[77] and what is more will go on calling the tune even when the War is over. That the centre of the poem is indeed about language and power is undeniable. The comedy is, as Hill suggests, an articulation of '"dumb insolence"' – [78]

> I smiled, as politely replied
> 'I'm afraid not, Sir.'

If so, then how far might this be disobedience of a 'Lawful Order' and as such a capital offence? Hill rightly draws our attention to the *tone* here because it constitutes the bizarre battlefield at the poem's centre. The politesse of the voice with its 'finicking accent' is outmanoeuvred by the first person's equally fastidious tongue: 'I'm afraid not, Sir'. Was it, after all, an order? 'Do you think you might crawl through there . . .' For even if there wasn't a hole, if the order was to crawl then crawl you did. There is a disturbing dimension of game to all this which seems irreconcilable with the reality around it. What accent should be given to 'I'm afraid not, Sir'? Gloucester? And if the reported speech (Gurney's own?) is articulated thus, what of the narrative voice? Is that 'regional' or rather just as Received in its pronunciation as the 'finicking accent'? Certainly the consciousness of class/linguistic determinations is essential to the meaning. For 'The Silent One' – he who

> chattered through
> Infinite lovely chatter of Bucks accent

– was, in truth, a 'noble fool, faithful to his stripes'. Stepping over, he had gone. Rather than politely reply, presumably he had silently accepted, and so now was infinite in his silence.

If 'The Silent One' should be read within a wound-up consciousness of class and power – calling the tune – we shouldn't let that overlook the poem's final drama. The conflicts and contrasts of voices play out the social drama and by extension the existential options – be silent and go; talk and refuse – within an assertion of moral values and their role during the destruction of all possible meaning. The end of the poem is about a set of absolutes each converging but not controlling the other: 'thought of music', 'swore deep heart's deep oaths' – these are desperate responses to the whizzing sounds of death. If, this time, it is best to keep up one's insolent servility ('Polite to God') just in case, it is nonetheless true, for all that, there is no escape from the totality of the moment. Agreed, one had refused the invitation to crawl forward and rather deemed retreat the answer but, as the last line suggests, however often you pull back there is still the overriding ultimate command to go forward – 'and a second time faced the screen'. The conclusion is grimly to the point. The 'screen' is the creeping barrage laid down as the infantry advance towards the enemy's lines; a refusal to follow the 'screen' (and the word is surely ironically conclusive: something which guards; keeps from sight; protects) silent on the page but in reality a barrage of terrifying noise (sound beyond sense) would indeed be 'cowardice before the enemy' and a capital offence. So there is no way out: the screen must be faced.

Behind this, then, is a brutal sense of the lines between fear or funk, choices about survival or numb fatalism. The surface of the poem – the dramatic exchange at its middle – is conscious of the depths: how can you face the 'screen'? The 'screen' hems you in, captures you and says – cross this land behind me or else. And how do you counter that? By saying no? Or running away?

A soldier who refused to go up to the front must have realized that he ran a very grave risk of being executed, for disobedience in itself was a capital offence. On 26 October a battalion of a London regiment which was in reserve in the Passchendaele sector had received orders to advance forthwith and to take up position in the line. While the rest of his company was falling in ready to move off Private S declined to leave his dugout. Both the adjutant and the regimental sergeant-major were called to the scene and they found S sitting on the ground with his rifle and equipment at his side. They told him repeatedly to go on parade and warned him of the consequences of his continued refusal, but he would neither move nor reply and eventually he was placed under close arrest. S was court-marshaled in November for 'disobeying an order in such a manner as to show willful defiance of authority'. It came out at his trial that he had been called up in February 1916, soon after the introduction of conscription. He was posted to France in January 1917 and had been a company stretcher-bearer during the heavy fighting in the spring and summer. He had borne a very good military character and had always carried out his duties in a satisfactory manner until the middle of August when he was awarded three months' Field Punishment Number One by his commanding officer for disobedience of an order. S told the court that he had seen so many terrible sights on the Western Front that they had affected his mind and he was no longer accountable for his behaviour. A captain in the RAMC gave evidence that he had spoken to S for ten minutes and had found no sign of mental deficiency or mental derangement. S was sentenced to death and he was shot two weeks before Christmas.[79]

X

I died in hell –
(They called it Passchendaele). My wound was slight,
And I was hobbling back; and then a shell
Burst slick upon the duck-boards: so I fell
Into the bottomless mud, and lost the light.[80]

Ypres: Ivor Gurney contrived not to suffer Passchendaele itself – but he made St. Julien. Having survived the Somme in December of 1916 and even the Arras fiasco (which did for Edward Thomas at 7:36 a.m., exactly, on April 9th, Easter Monday) by being wounded in the arm on Good Friday, the first day of the attack, it seemed he had that talent Napoleon required of a General – luck. Up to a point; for the debacle at Arras under Nivelle's vain and grossly incompetent leadership had resulted in, first, the utter demoralization of the French Army and, second, the postponement of Haig's grand plan for the Ypres Salient. As for the first:

One regiment being led to the front went docilely enough, but persisted in baa-ing like sheep to indicate that they were lambs being driven to slaughter. When reprimanded by their commanding officer, the mutineers simply returned to the rest billets from which they had come. An artillery regiment tried to blow up the Schneider-Creusot munitions works. One general was severely beaten; 21,174 Frenchmen deserted outright. Unit after unit refused duty. Officers who tried to use force on the recalcitrant men were killed or beaten. Trains were derailed. Strikes and riots broke out in the domestic interior. A total of fifty-four divisions – at least three-quarters of a million fighting men – were involved. [81]

Pétain succeeded the megalomaniac Nivelle five weeks after the Arras campaign had ground its hapless way to a standstill: *esprit de corps* was immediately restored with the official shooting of twenty-three mutineers on the one hand and, on the other, the annihilation by French artillery of two hundred and fifty more.[82] If the British Army avoided such traumatic outbursts of popular discontent it must have been due, one supposes, to the policy of continuously encouraging the others: averaged out, from 1914 to 1920 one man a week was shot for some breach of military law or other: that is, a total of 346. We should bear this in mind when we consider what took place near St. Julien in September – the threat of punishment must have been in men's minds as they weighed up their existential choices: 'dithipline'. Certainly something other than *esprit de corps* must have intimidated the troops to go on sinking beneath the mire of Haig's stubborn plan. On July 31st – and for the following three days and nights – it rained. In theory, having been penned within the Ypres salient since the first months of the War, the British and Commonwealth troops were still ready to burst through the German lines and clear a route for the cavalry to slash their way across the plains of Flanders to the Belgian coast. Thus would the German Army be outflanked and thus – at a stroke – would Haig become the greatest man who ever lived. In practice, the combination of incessant rain, clay, high water tables and massive bombardments by Haig's own artillery turned the earth into an impassable morass and an unimaginable nightmare. There were two hundred and fifty thousand Allied casualties, one third of whom were dead[83] and another third 'missing': which simply meant 'they had been blown to unrecognizable fragments, drowned or suffocated in liquid mud'.[84] Ypres: the high summer and autumn of 1917.

A party of 'A' Company men passing up to the front line found . . . a man bogged to above the knees. The united efforts of four of them with rifles beneath his armpits, made not the slightest impression, and to dig, even if shovels had been available, would be impossible, for there was no foothold. Duty compelled them to move on up to the line, and when two days later they passed down that way the wretched fellow was still there; but only his head was now visible and he was raving mad.[85]

The moment you set off you felt that dreadful suction. It was forever pulling you down, and you could hear the sound of your feet coming out in a kind of sucking 'plop' that seemed much louder at night when you were on your own. In a way, it was worse when the mud didn't suck you down; when it yielded under your feet you knew that it was a body you were treading on. It was terrifying. You'd tread on one on the stomach, perhaps, and it would grunt all the air out of its body. It made your hair stand on end. The smell could make you vomit. And you could always tell whether it was a dead Jerry or a dead Tommy. The Germans smelt different in death.[86]

'When windy "write letters" and so – here you are' – thus Ivor Gurney to Marion Scott on August 31st. 'For Fritz has been shelling and it has rattled me'.[87] The letters from Ypres attempt to keep a grip – but even away from the line the shelling went on. The conversation is about his own poetry – the forthcoming *Severn and Somme* – and that of others. But the truth is that he was in 'A country like the last Hell of desolation'.[88] On August 21st, the Gloucesters had gone into the line; the next day, together with the Oxford and Bucks, they launched an attack upon 'a giant concrete fortress known as Pond Farm. The exact part that Gurney played in these and subsequent battles is not known'.[89] Nevertheless, we can perhaps understand something of that particular battle through the diaries of Edwin Vaughan, a subaltern with the Warwicks who went into line with the Gloucesters. His account takes us into the pits of hopelessness:

> I found the CO waiting for me and I sat down in the mud beside him feeling dead beat and horribly ill. What he was saying I had no idea, for I must have fainted or gone to sleep. After what seemed a long time I heard a voice saying unintelligible things, and I was just able to mutter, 'I'm awfully sorry, Sir, but I haven't the least idea what you're saying.' He shook me violently and said 'Now, Vaughan, pull yourself together.' Whereupon I was alert in a moment and he repeated his instructions. I was

to form up my platoons in depth to the right of where we were then sitting. The Gloucesters were going out before dawn and the following night I was to spread out to the left and form a line joining the Ox and Bucks. Then he left me and I sat for a while staring into the darkness, realizing that we were in a hell of a place. [90]

Indeed a 'hell of a place': 'A country like the last Hell of desolation' – over and over witnesses saw the Salient through that word.

> S' io avessi le rime aspre e chiocce,
>   come si converrebbe al tristo buco,
>   sopra il qual pontan tutte l' altre rocce,
>
> io premerei di mio concetto il suco
>   più pienamente; ma perch' io non l' abbo,
>   non senza tema a dicer mi conduco:
>
> chè non è impresa da pigliare a gabbo
>   descriver fondo a tutto l' universo,
>   nè da lingua che chiami mamma e babbo.
>
>   (Canto XXXII)

> If I had rhymes rough and hoarse, as would
>   befit the dismal hole, on which all the other
>   rocky steeps converge and weigh,
>
> I should press out the juice of my conception
>   more fully; but since I have them not, not
>   without fear I bring myself to tell thereof:
>
> for to describe the bottom of all the Universe is
>   not an enterprise for being taken up in sport,
>   nor for a tongue that cries mamma and papa.[91]

But here is 'a young officer, 1917' struggling through the nightmare of the battle of Langemark: August 27 and these are the experiences he records in his diary – barely beyond childhood but now the language of 'mamma e babbo' far far beyond recall:

Up the road we staggered, shells bursting around us. A man stopped dead in front of me, and exasperated I cursed him and butted him with my knee. Very gently he said 'I'm blind,

Sir,' and turned to show me his eyes and nose torn away by a piece of shell. 'Oh God! I'm sorry, sonny,' I said. 'Keep going on the hard part,' and left him staggering back in his darkness. At the Triangle the shelling was lighter and the rifle fire far above our heads. Around us were numerous dead, and in shell-holes where they had crawled to safety were wounded men.

. . .

From the darkness on all sides came the groans and wails of wounded men; faint, long, sobbing moans of agony, and despairing shrieks. It was too horribly obvious that dozens of men with serious wounds must have crawled for safety into new shell-holes, and now the water was rising about them and, powerless to move, they were slowly drowning. [92]

And the end of all that – having taken the enemy's pill box and being relieved – back behind the lines at Brigade Head-quarters with fifteen out of the original ninety men of 'D' Company left alive, Vaughan returned to his tent to write out the casualty report. Instead '[f]eeling sick and lonely . . . I sat on the floor and drank whisky after whisky as I gazed into a black and empty future'.[93] For it was by no means over, the battle of Ypres: its conclusion came only when the Canadians entered Passchendaele village three months later on November 6th. Even so one feels that the future lying bleakly before him was not only the sound and fury but the signified nothing: life? What is that?

The following day Lieutenant-General Sir Launcelot Kiggell paid his first visit to the fighting zone. As his staff car lurched through the swamp land and neared the battleground he became more and more agitated. Finally he burst into tears and muttered, 'Good God, did we really send men to fight in that?'

The man beside him, who had been through the campaign, replied tonelessly, 'It's worse further on up.'[94]

Edwin Campion Vaughan, nineteen, survived Langemark and the Third Battle of Ypres – up to a point. For although he became a Captain and won an M.C., he could not 'settle down in civilian life'[95] and after an unsuccessful post-war career in the R.A.F. was invalided out. He died at the age of thirty-four.

XI

Survival? What did it mean?

                    The more monstrous
        fate
Shadows our own, the mind swoons doubly burdened,
Taught how for miles our anguish groans and bleeds,
A whole sweet countryside amuck with murder;
Each moment puffed into a year with death.[96]

'The mind swoons doubly burdened'. Blunden's sense of the tor-
tures in survival might seem secondary when put next to the
unspeakable miseries of those who drowned in that whole sweet
countryside amuck with death; nonetheless it meant controlling
one's own experiences which are the experiences of watching and
hearing those who have sunk below the filth (the head raving mad
in its slow burial alive, suffocated as it is sucked down screaming):
this is the burden of continuance. Some survive survival. Some
do not.

        They gave me to Hell black torture as surely
        As God – if He judge them – shall judge for it.
        They tortured my last nerve, and tortured my wit.[97]

'They' shall be judged: 'they' who made men make this War
because 'they' have left men mad to have survived; mad not to
have died:

                O Tan-Faced Prairie Boy

. . .

A Company almost of true friends tried to the courage ends –
The dead with living equal – and living lucky alone,
(Having taken Dead Man's many chances and still for other ones)
A verse of love for you –

. . .

Love endless for you – though I win to rapt, and mapped
Music, and to my deep thought get great sound shaped.
You knew my mind – what it hoped – not to keep body unhurt,
Nor to save life so much as to return to the heart;
To find my heart again in some candle-lit room

And work out music till the true shape and soul should come.
I left not you – why have you left me to fall
Into the hands of evil lying lies to the truth of Hell.
(I was a war poet, England bound to honour by Her blood)
Why have you dead ones not saved me – you dead ones not helped
    well?
Or is it even Michail, my master, strict; forbidding a good?
But why you, Gloucesters, O dead ones, my dear companions,
Laventie – Vermand – Ypres, why have you not given
Courage from beyond the grave to your comrade so driven
By torment from his heart to call for you, friends under the guns?

Is there not honour of war poet at rebirth, or in Heaven? [98]

'A verse of love for you', Gurney describes it and following on from
Whitman there is at first sight a dimension of the homoerotic in his
guilty lament.

O Tan-Faced Prairie-Boy

O tan-faced prairie-boy,
Before you came to camp came many a welcome gift,
Praises and presents came and nourishing food, till at last
    among the recruits,
You came, taciturn, with nothing to give – we but look'd on
    each other,
When lo! more than all the gifts of the world you gave me.[99]

But again, perhaps not: insofar as Whitman's poem is a celebration
of the male community of the war, Gurney may be said to express
something of the same intensity. What charges Whitman's verse is
that thrill of sensuality which is coded for us in the words 'gift' and
'give': the physicality of the 'Boy' is in the title and the silence he
creates – 'taciturn'. We are persuaded that the democracy of desire
transcends linguistic complications. The face is a face to be looked
at. The power of giving up oneself is balanced between aggression
and passivity: the regard is mutual; 'look'd on/each other'. The
gift then transforms the single stare into a vision of life, 'gifts
of the world'. Gurney's poem deliberately appropriates the title
in order to make us conscious of male love, but love of what
might be called the spiritual virtue of the physical: courage.

A Company almost of true friends tried to the courage ends –
The dead with living equal. . .
A verse of love for you –

'Love endless for you . . . I left not you – why have you left
me . . .'. We have at last arrived. From the oblique subversions
of 'Bohemians' or 'The Silent One' – their ironies and reservations – we have in this an example of the confession which haunts
and torments Gurney. He survived to be left with memories of
those who showed the nerve to stick it out – 'never disgraced'.
The guilt of survival we know about in its general shape and
form – Graves, Sassoon, Blunden – but in Ivor Gurney's case it
seems to be acute to the point of insufferable torment. We are
aware – following the sequence of his later poems – that there
is a 'story', one which Gurney was unable to forget or tell
straight; a story of nerve and courage; of surviving by having
the instinct to survive; by saying 'No'. No more. He survived
Third Ypres – Passchendaele – by getting out. And that became
his tragedy.

XII

'Gas brought England, and some hope – fulfilling'.[100] Hurd comments: 'An element of mystery attaches itself not only to the date
on which Ivor Gurney was gassed, but also to the degree to which
he was affected'.[101] For, as Hurd further observes, his letters back
to England seem to suggest that it was all pretty small beer:

By the way I am still in the line, but not having at all a bad
time of it. My throat is sore from gas; it is just (or was) as if I
had had catarrh, but only an occasional explosion of coughing
is left now. No luck! One cannot smell the new gas. One starts
sneezing. The old gas had a heavy hothouse Swinburnian filthy
sort of odour – voluptuous and full of danger.[102]

And later: 'Being gassed (mildly) with the new gas is no worse than
catarrh or a bad cold'.[103] So how did it come about that Gurney got
a Blighty – by the twenty-sixth of September was writing to Marion
Scott from Ward 24, Edinburgh War Hospital, Bangour, Scotland?

Hurd quotes, without comment, one of the uncollected poems in the context of this 'mystery': perhaps these lines point towards what appears to be the 'truth'.

> – yet gas changed all;
> Instead of moving South with the Fifth Army,
> Chokes and gasps of gas moved a doctor's sympathy
> (Three weeks in needing rest – hoping a week to befall)
> And got to Blighty – as unexpectedly as ever any
> Of honest gas (but not much) got by a tale
> Of five hours gas bombardment, which was true
> (I brought that down) or keeping silence as to the
> Real reason – which was three weeks at Ypres,
> Without a rest (or laurel) (nor yet a cypress),
> Having seen a Passchendaele lit with a flare of fire
> And Ypres a dawn light ruddy and golden of desire,
> The stuck tanks – and shook at our guns going in
> As my body would not stay still at such Hell of din;
> Worse than any of theirs . . .
> . . .
>
> Death was compelled a hundred times and withheld,
> Yet there is no honour of Ypres – though the Romans had
> Saluted Ypres the word – without word gainsaid
> They bent my helmet for me; they broke the machine gun nearly,
> Carefully ranging, traversing, till the gun was tilted
> Which after setting upright we set tobacco alight.[104]

'The real reason'. The real reason was – simply – enough: enough was enough. There is no honour of Ypres and besides 'they bent my helmet for me'. It seems to be that truth which Gurney slides through in this last letter to Marion Scott from the Casualty Clearing Station – 21 September, 1919 (sic) – which, recall, would have passed beneath the censor's eye:

> I am very sorry the proofs will reach you in so dirty an envelope. Your own, but it had travelled, and such things must be shoved any old where in the Army. Curse the Army!
>   This is an annoying wind; it gathers or seems to gather the sweetest things one has ever known to drift about and taunt a poor private of no renown at all, at all. Curse the wind!
>   By the way, I moi meme have got the name for being extremely

cool under shell-fire. It may be so to the view, but could they read my mind sometimes! So you see, neurasthenia leads one to a strange praise. By conquering fear-of-Life one may learn at once to love Life and to scorn death together; but neither has come yet in reality.

With best wishes: Your sincere friend   Ivor Gurney [105]

The very mention of 'neurasthenia' seems provocative. Fussell's analysis [106] of letters from the front suggests a kind of uniform, standard, style due, in the main, to the fact of censorship. What would be made of the literary musical private who knew how to choose his words? Did he imagine the risks of 'dithipline' as he manoeuvered his doubtful way back? For it seems – through the mass of words he would go on to write – that underneath the cool Gurney believed he had funked it. Indeed, even before the end of the War, writing to Marion Scott about his possible movements, knowing well that he might still be sent back to France, he dares confess to 'a bit of luck; owing to slight indigestion (presumably due to gas; wink, wink!).'[107] A wangler? A malingerer?

XIII

But at this moment of a carefully constructed personal story, we must place Gurney in another context, beyond the terrible self-contempt of his own image; for clearly in the Asylum's solitude he brooded over that moment at Ypres – wracked by his faith in companionship, his love, of the courageous who stayed and died. We have to understand not simply the pathology of one soul but its life within the reality of the mass of twentieth century European men who survived the War. For it is evident that Gurney's references to the 'new gas' are not the least misleading of his confessions about Ypres and that his self-pity and self-contempt – the double-self judging and loathing; explaining itself against itself – were far from warranted. There were two major innovations to the art of warfare at Ypres – one on each side. The British introduced massed tanks as a major assault weapon – they sank into the mud and were useless. The Germans, on the other hand, had better luck: 'The debut of mustard gas was dramatic and the first effects sensational'. On the night of 12th-13th of July 50,000 mustard gas shells were fired into the area between St. Jean and Potijze just east of Ypres:

At the front and in the rear there were many casualties, but most were not severely injured. The alarming feature was the partial blindness of the casualties who also suffered from progressive conjunctivitis. It says a great deal for the morale and the discipline of the men that there was no panic, and somehow they were quickly guided to the CCS where doctors and nurses treated the unusual and indeed, alarming symptoms as well as they could. C. G. Douglas . . . noted on his rounds that the men were rapidly developing blisters on buttocks, genitals, and armpits. In his report of 14 July he surmised that the Germans had fired some skin-irritating substance. But two days later many of the casualties were suffering from bronchitis and a few had died from inflammation of the lungs. The course of the infection and the aetiology of the disease were worrying because they followed no pattern and the delayed action of the poison was unheard of. By 18 July the eyes were generally improving, but the pulmonary symptoms remained severe. Six days later the sick still had bronchitis and noticeable skin rashes instead of blisters, but the conjunctivitis had disappeared.[108]

The effects of mustard gas poisoning – 'pain, fear, skin inflammations, embarrassment'[109] – are notable in their curiously unpleasant mix of the psychic and somatic. As a result it became clear that the effect on the whole man was complex, inducing, not least, depression and war weariness. For, apart from the immediate explosion, there were the lingering dangers of the gas: it clung to the ground and to textiles and leather. Given all this, it is important to note L. F. Haber's research into particular responses to mustard gas: talking to Chelsea Pensioners his overall impression was first, of the chanciness of the gas and second, the diversity of men's reactions to it. Thus one victim recalled that although he breathed in some gas he was not burnt but did suffer from catarrh and bronchitis. On the other hand, the Commanding Officer, 'was evacuated, blinded and never returned'.[110] Now consider Haber on the general experience of mustard-gas:

Conjunctivitis, painful and briefly frightening, was, by far, the commonest injury caused by mustard gas – 86 per cent of the USA gas casualties experienced it – but also the least dangerous. It yielded after three or four days to boracic washes or colloidal silver in aqueous solution and disappeared entirely in ten days to a fortnight. Conjunctivitis by itself rarely led to complications but was a good indicator of the severity of the other injuries. One might say that the worse the state of the eyes, the worse would be the blisters and the inflammation of the mucous membranes. Early and accurate diagnosis of the extent of exposure, careful handling at the blistering stage, and good nursing throughout determined the course of the illness. At first the patient would look as if he was suffering from scarlet fever, then the rash turned into blisters which took up to four weeks to break. If the blisters became infected, which was common, the patient might take another five to six weeks to recover. This stage of the treatment called for careful nursing and frequent changes of dressings. Skin creams based on animal fats, much favoured by the French, were to be avoided. . . . Zinc oxide cream, hydrogen peroxide compresses, talcum powder, vaseline . . . were of some use, but the best treatment consisted of keeping the blisters aseptic, covering them lightly, and avoiding friction. These were counsels of perfection for the most tender parts of the body such as buttocks, genitals, armpits, and ears were often inflamed by contact with mustard gas. As the patient usually could not renew dressings or compresses himself, mustard-gas burns called for simple but meticulous care and when it was lacking, recovery took that much longer. The inflammation of the throat presented the greatest potential danger and was usually followed by bronchitis which, in those days, called for frequent balsam inhalations. If the weather was mild and dry and the staff competent, the burns and the throat would clear in anything from four to six weeks, a little longer in difficult cases. But if bronchitis developed into pneumonia or worse, the patient was at risk and death from mustard gas, which ranged from 1 to 3 per cent of the cases, was due invariably to pulmonary complications. Douglas, a careful observer of mustard-gas injury from July 1917 onwards, was of the opinion that a very large proportion of the cases could be 'fit for duty in four to six weeks', which included one week in a convalescent depot and two to three weeks' light drill and 'recuperation' in a rest camp. This timetable applied to those whose exposure had been mild – perhaps some blisters and slight throat inflammation.[111]

This may make us pause. If we recall Ivor Gurney's own account of gas, within the context of both verse and prose accounts of the experience, the temptation is to feel even more strongly that he was faking it. For, again, if – as he asserts – it was indeed the 'new' gas which had done for him, the lack of certain dominant (if not necessary) symptoms is striking: why are there no references to burns or conjunctivitis? The singular omission of precise description – *pace* the censor – seems remarkable. 'One cannot smell the new gas'.[112] But according to Haber, mustard-gas gave off a smell of garlic or else 'English mustard' – obviously. There could be a danger here, however, of being too sceptical. Certainly, a comparison of Gurney's casual recollection of his experience – 'One starts sneezing'[113] – with possibly the most famous account of a gas attack, Owen's 'Dulce et Decorum Est', might lead us to dismiss the common cold when the apparent fact was a death by hanging:

> . . . the white eyes writhing in his face,
> His hanging face, like a devil's sick of sin;
> If you could hear, at every jolt, the blood
> Come gargling from the froth-corrupted lungs,
> Obscene as cancer, bitter as the cud
> Of vile, incurable sores on innocent tongues, – [114]

But, in truth, this merely confirms the depth of the mystery: according to Haber, Owen is here describing a chlorine attack whose symptoms were dramatically different from mustard gas.[115]

There seem to be three possible explanations then – none of them necessarily exclusive. First, we might accept the mustard-gas theory and conclude that Gurney suffered an extremely mild case – so mild that almost none of the most conspicuous symptoms appeared. If so, the only explanation for the subsequent Blighty can lie with the novelty of the attack: doctors at the Casualty Clearing Station might have been sufficiently confused to have passed a patient who hitherto might have been rejected. In this case, the second possibility shades into the first. It may well have been true that Gurney was by this time genuinely neurasthenic – depression and fatigue suddenly finding a convenient objective correlative. As he admits, there was every reason to want out: he had 'marched from Somme to St / Quentin, / Got wounded, saw Rouen, Arras';[116] had been a machine-gunner (and thus at greater risk) and now at Ypres survived shrapnel: '[L]ast night on fatigue I had the roughest chanciest hour I ever had. My shrapnel helmet has an interesting dent in it.'[117] In short, he had endured three years and now there was cause enough to take a chance: 'three weeks at Ypres'.[118] In which case, the rest of his life would be haunted by the knowledge – 'wink, wink' – of funking it: that would be the terrible truth. How could one be the poet of War; of love for the fallen; of companionship in courage if, after all, it had ended with a wangle? Any soldier with his share of an intense sense of self-respect would tragically have prepared, at the moment of escape, for a subsequent career of isolation and madness. And yet it is precisely such a self-perception which, ironically, might have precluded him from the third possibility. If it was, as he insisted, 'honest gas' even as deflatingly he parenthetically admits '(but not much)',[119] then the attack might not have been mustard at all; it might very well have been phosgene. In 1916, the gas shell replaced the cloud and instead of chlorine, phosgene was introduced. The arsenical gas was, in fact, far more insidious than either its predecessor, chlorine, or the later, more dramatic, innovation of Ypres:

> For up to two or three hours, sometimes longer, the casualty suffered little or no discomfort. Thereafter, by which time the man was on his way to or already at the CCS, his condition would deteriorate very quickly with symptoms of general collapse and tendency to circulation failure from drowning of the lungs.[120]

It smelled 'faintly of silage and, unlike chlorine, inhalation causes no spasm'.[121] Despite the fact of the victim's subsequent immediate deterioration, the initial recovery from phosgene – it had none of the dramatic external symptoms of mustard gas – was strong. With good nursing (absolute rest, warmth, a light diet, plenty of fluid and regular oxygen treatment[122]) physiological recovery appeared complete. However, the long-term effects of phosgene were far more insidious than the doctors or their patients at first realized. For victims in time became spiritually debilitated: they experienced depression and war-weariness; '"intense mental distress . . . utter dejection and hopeless misery"':[123] the psychic trauma was deep and long-lasting. It, furthermore, seems to have been related to the long-term physical debilitation many victims also suffered. Minds and bodies respond in different ways, certainly (see Haber, Ch.9, *passim*): nonetheless, like thousands of other soldiers, Ivor Gurney carried unseen wounds out of the war, both psychic and somatic; wounds which would dominate the mind and the body in his terrible struggle to survive bleak peace-time life:

Men who had lost limbs or their faculties were easy enough
to identify, to compensate, and to sympathize with, but those
hurt by gas presented unusual problems, for even when their
symptoms were precisely classified, to what extent were they due
to poison gas or to other factors? It was found that following the
Armistice the strain relaxed, and as the tension eased so sickness
became pronounced: the influenza pandemic hospitalized scores
of thousands and, quite independently, extreme fatigue emerged
as a major, if short-lived post-war development, called by the British 'neurasthenic disablement'. These illnesses often displayed
the same symptoms which characterized those who had been
gassed, treated, and returned to duty, or – in more serious
cases – discharged as unfit. They easily fell victim to bronchitis,
tended to asthma, and were often off work with throat or lung
infections. Their 'wind was gone' and their hearts were 'irritable'
as Macpherson was to describe it later, and the diagnosis DAH
for disordered action of the heart was widely used as a catch-all
for an undefined and unsatisfactory condition. Douglas, who
had examined hundreds of gassed, wrote to Hartley after the
war that few of those who survived gas 'exhibit in the end
serious, morbid lesions'; some, however, continued to suffer
from 'indefinite symptoms' of which he remarked: 'I fancy there
is a good deal of the neurasthenic element in many of these DAH
cases.' It was realized quite early that some of the sick had had a
history of chest diseases and should not have been called up, or
if called up, not exposed to gas. But by 1919 that was water under
the bridge, and in any case the immediate difficulty was caused
by the demobilized soldier's work or environment. A severe gas
injury left a man less able to cope with a tiring job in a dusty
or humid atmosphere: the damp, cheerless, smoky winters of
industrial England, northern France, or the Ruhr soon rendered
the ex-soldiers, many of them cigarette-smokers, unfit. Bronchitis
was then a common illness, often associated with pulmonary
infections, and it strained the heart muscle. There was also the
danger that, as with tuberculosis, heavy, deep coughing would
reopen scar tissue and lead to bleeding.[124]

So: possibly gassed, possibly neurasthenic – probably both but full
of self-doubt and contempt – ultimately Gurney made his way
home where, twenty years after Ypres, he died, a heavy smoker, of
tuberculosis.

XIV

War Books

What did they expect of our toil and extreme
Hunger – the perfect drawing of a heart's dream?
Did they look for a book of wrought art's perfection,
Who promised no reading, nor praise, nor publication?
Out of the heart's sickness the spirit wrote
For delight, or to escape hunger, or of war's worst anger,
When the guns died to silence and men would gather sense
Somehow together, and find this was life indeed,
And praise another's nobleness, or to Cotswold get hence.
There we wrote – Corbie Ridge – or in Gonnehem at rest –
Or Fauquissart – our world's death songs, ever the best.[125]

   An analysis of war experience must confront directly this experience of being 'made' strange. An examination of the identities formed in war must come to terms with the fact that these identities were formed beyond the margins of normal social experience. This was precisely what made them so lasting, so immune to erosion by the routines of postwar social and economic life, and so difficult to grasp with the traditional tools of sociological and psychological analysis.[126]

And in writing of their war experiences, these men were not primarily articulating a 'literature of warning' but rather one of 'bereavement', first, and 'guilt' second.[127] Not to mention indignation, third. Their writing is pervaded by feelings of 'marginality, of separation from a civilian world to which it seemed impossible to return'.[128] But equally we are talking about a mass of particular human experiences made literature; the multiple 'plain' man of C. E. Montague's *Disenchantment*, who survived no end of stunts, strafes and simple inconvenient hard work to discover

> [e]very disease which victory was to cure . . . raging worse than before: more poverty, less liberty, more likelihood of other wars, more spite between master and man, less national comradeship.[129]

This is the language of educated 'disenchantment', 1922. At the

centre of men's experience, then, is a profound sense of being creatures on the margin. Now the soldier returns as the estranged – that
mythic creature – bearing memories of his polluting experiences:
filth and ordure, exploding brains, rotting entrails, bloated rats,
severed limbs and heads. His true kinship is with the defeated
enemy not the victorious folk. As the years distanced the experiences, it became clear that the 'psychoneurotic diseases of war
proved to be more enduring, and more expensive to treat, than
physical ailments'.[130] Which may help to explain the lag between
the end of the war and the accounts and recollections that began
to appear in the mid-twenties. Things were being worked out;
we are familiar with the psychic pathologies now. Equally we
should not forget the further dimension to the returned warrior's
trauma: if over the last four or more years his world had been
recreated, making of him not only an automatized killer but
also a will-less labourer, how was he to be reintegrated within
an economy and class structure which had succeeded very well
without him?

> Even to lead a laden mule in the dark over waste ground
> confusingly wired and trenched is work; to get him back on to
> his feet when fallen and wriggling, in wild consternation, among
> a tangle of old barbed wire may be quite hard work.
>   . . .
>   After four days of their labours as sumpter mules, or muleteers,
> the company would plod back for another four days of duty in
> trenches, come out yet more universally tired at their end, and
> drift back to rest-billets, out of ordinary shell-fire, for their sixteen
> days or 'divisional rest.' Here their work was really lighter, but still
> it was work and not rest. It did not wholly wind up in most of
> the men the spring that had run down while they were in the
> line. And then the division would go again into the line, and
> the old cycle be worked through once more. So most of the
> privates were tired the whole of the time; sometimes to the
> point of torment, sometimes much less, but always more or less
> tired.[131]

But now what were they good for? In 1922 – the year Ivor Gurney
was irrecoverably committed to the asylum – unemployment rose
from its 1920 level of 3.1 per cent to 13.8 per cent.[132] No job and,
worse, no home – that was the fact of his existence. He was among
the losers. And this meant that his relations with other members

of the Gurney family were highly complicated. For, first, the status of the family itself was unstable. If, as it seems, the historical orthodoxy holds that by '1919 . . . Britain contained a working class with a greater sense of cohesion than had been the case in the past' [133] where did that leave the Gurneys? Ivor's father, as a tailor before the war, would presumably have felt apart from the unskilled labouring class; one effect however of wartime mass-recruitment and intense industrial transformations had been to diminish the role of the self-employed artisan. David Gurney died in 1919: one son, Ronald, continued the tradition of skilled manual craft, but Ivor Gurney's two sisters certainly had other things in mind. Winifred became a nurse; Dorothy a secretary and teacher.[134] So how were they, not to mention the put-upon Ronald, going to tolerate the unemployed unhoused sibling who, before the war, had left the sure confines of provincial life for cosmopolitan glamour? For, second, by becoming an 'artist' – the famous composer – Ivor had removed himself from the family structure, creating, automatically the romantic figure of the deracinated creative genius beyond the nice complications of the English class system. And now, four years after the War, struggling as they were to keep themselves ahead of the rising working classes, profiting at last from deflation and reduced taxation, what was a family with artisan roots and middle class aspirations to make of the hostile, embittered, unwell, unemployed, unhoused, soldier-musician-poet?

He began to imagine that 'electrical tricks' were being played on him. He felt pains in the head and the voices returned. He left his aunt's house and thrust himself, uninvited, on his brother, who had just married. Here his behaviour became intolerable. He would shut himself in the front room of their house in Worcester Street and shout for them to keep away. He would sit with a cushion on his head to guard against electric waves coming from the wireless. He refused to go to bed, or to eat properly. He sneered at his brother's orthodoxies: 'Only fools go to work – why dont you get somebody else to keep you.' He flew into violent rages. He threatened suicide and called at the police station to demand a revolver. He was given sedatives by the doctor, but swallowed the lot as soon as his back was turned. He tried to gas himself.

Distraught, the family appealed to the doctors again and they in turn called in the two magistrates necessary for committal.

There was no alternative. By the middle of September 1922, Ivor
Gurney appeared to be insane. [135]

His brother, Ronald, years earlier, 'had dreamed of becoming a
doctor, but such money as the family could spare had gone
automatically to Ivor's education'.[136] So now, like his father forced
to make do as a tailor, he had Ivor, four years his senior, committed
in September, 1922.

XV

Sonnet – September 1922

Fierce indignation is best understood by those
Who have time or no fear, or a hope in its real good.
One loses it with a filed soul or in sentimental mood.
Anger is gone with sunset, or flows as flows
The water in easy mill-runs; the earth that ploughs
Forgets protestation in its turning, the rood
Prepares, considers, fulfils; and the poppy's blood
Makes old the old changing of the headland's brows.

But the toad under the harrow toadiness
Is known to forget, and even the butterfly
Has doubts of wisdom when that clanking thing goes by
And's not distressed. A twisted thing keeps still –
That thing easier twisted than a grocer's bill –
And no history of November keeps the guy.[137]

'Fierce indignation' – that is one way to describe it. Perhaps
resentment is a meaner qualification of the emotions that tortured
the man. Resentment at the war; resentment at the peace – made
mad by the circumstances of his life. But of course the paradox
of the poem's form and the writer's state of mind is always with
us. Silkin, in writing of Gurney's resentment, asks if he had 'not
become intermittently mad, would anyone have thought to say that
[this poetry] was the expression of someone deranged?'[138] We are
brought here to that question most enigmatically formulated by
Eliot in *The Waste Land*: how can incoherence be articulated other
than coherently? And, of course, it cannot: an answer otherwise

succumbs to the fallacy of imitative form. And yet, here, with Ivor Gurney we have the sonnet's sestet apparently breaking its meaning down even as the octave has, after all, asserted control and the rightness of healing. The poem seems to inhabit, simultaneously, meaningless and articulate worlds. The loss of indignation is, at first, understood as a creative process, a subsumption within the *world* (Silkin again is right to remind us of the profound importance of nature for Gurney's sane art) and its life of growth within loss. Sunset; mill-runs; the ploughed earth: yet even as the language of the poem is to all appearances calm, quiet, it is simultaneously straining, calmly and quietly enough, against a tendency to violence

> . . . the rood
> Prepares, considers, fulfils; and the poppy's blood
> Makes old the old changing of the headland's brows.

The rood is, of course, the measurement of the field (forty rods) and the cross on which Christ died. The line leading up to it ('the earth that ploughs') may perhaps be citing Hopkins on the agony:

> No wonder of it: sheér plód makes plough down sillion
> Shine. . . [139]

And obviously the blood red of the poppy continues that thought while recalling France and its wounded earth. The problems begin with the sestet and here perhaps one is not initially prepared to accept the paradox of mad sanity. At best we might retrieve the position by arguing for an eccentricity of language.

> But the toad under the harrow toadiness
> Is known to forget . . .

But that won't really do: 'toadiness' has a confidence which forces us to recognize that an act of judgement is being called for. The word has no entry in the *O.E.D.* so we may want to accept that the essence of real – rather than human – toads is being evoked. On the other hand, the poem's syntax is asserting the essence of *human* toadiness: 'But' takes us back to the poem's beginning, that is, to 'Fierce indignation'. And of course, under the entry simply for 'toad' is, among the examples of its anthropomorphic meanings ('to

be a mean dependent, toady'), 'Toad under a harrow': attributed
to Bentham. Kipling – not cited – is even more to the point here:
'Pagett, M.P.' has as its epigraph this:

> The toad beneath the harrow knows
> Exactly where each tooth-point goes;
> The butterfly upon the road
> Teaches contentment to that toad.[140]

'Fierce indignation' – the toady, toad-eating, harrowed toad: 'toad-
eater' one who eats toads; the Charlatan's attendant 'employed to
eat toads (held to be poisonous) to enable his master to exhibit
his skill in expelling poison' (*O.E.D.*). So, here are all the human
characteristics even as Gurney keeps the toad literally there – the
connotations of subterranean, dark, trapped, furtive toads are sustained by the mind's eye dwelling on the real destructive harrow.
And yet this literalness – the materiality of the poem – serves to
sustain the conjunction of sestet with octave. The 'reality' of the land
and its toad is transformed while remaining stubbornly irreducible:
the toads also live/have lived in the octave, in the earth which
gushes with the poppies' blood. So, again, the 'real' toads are the
soldiers in the earth, dead, and in the trenches, awaiting it. The
harrowing plough is 'really' the harrowing hell of shellfire: the
harrow 'pulverizes' (*O.E.D.*) the earth. It is the harrow which actually
creates hell. But all this resentment, which had been transformed
from the seemingly calm order as the octave prepared to turn,

> . . . the rood
> Prepares, considers, fulfils . . .

is not confined to the harrow: unlike Kipling's butterfly safely upon
the road, teaching contentment, Gurney's creature has 'doubts of
wisdom'. 'Butterfly mind' – now that hears the 'clanking' harrow
and too late realizes it is 'not distressed'. So, 'they', they too
shall find out. The toads shall be stirred to fierce indignation;
the butterflies to the beginnings of knowledge. This is a poem
for our century: now we shall witness – all of us – the harrowing
of hell. Active victims and passive witnesses are all to be tortured
by the machine. Distress is no more: the relations of pain to mental
suffering, the growth of imagination, the capacity to feel for the
sacrifice of others – none of this can have meaning (how can it?) for

the machine. The man behind the machine – the man inside it – is invisible, beyond touch, beyond feelings. As the plough, so the tank grinding through the earth of No Man's Land, pulverizing life.

And so 'thing' becomes the key word:

> A twisted thing keeps still –

This is what has duly been crushed, churned up, harrowed (with the full senses of 'harrowing experiences') and is now – instead of, say, ugly toad or gilded butterfly – a 'twisted thing': still because lifeless. The mutilated thing is beyond or past indignation. The poem powerfully articulates its sense of moral and physical helplessness before the forces – the 'clanking things' – pulverizing life into 'twisted things'.

> That thing easier twisted than a grocer's bill –

This figure seems to be quite at odds with the cool cunning logic of the whole deep metaphor the sestet had hitherto so resolutely sustained: except that the twisted bill ironically points back to material reality – the earth – and conceptualizations of it via our fiduciary exchanges. On the one hand what is easier to twist than a grocer's bill? Flimsy paper, as insubstantial as – twist – that and hence so much for the poem's proud opening: 'Fierce indignation'. But, then again, where does paper come from? Is it not part of the whole process of destruction/creation with which the poem is obsessed? And groceries? Where but from the earth and its slaughterhouses; the earth which is, as it were, being harrowed by the cruel plough. There is a poem of the 1922–25 period which takes this matter to the extreme.

Of Cruelty

From the racked substance of the earth comes the plant and
That with heat and the night frost is tortured:
To some perfection that grows, man's thought wills his hand –
Roots rent, crown broken, grub-holed, it is drawn upward.

A hundred things since the first stir have hunted it,
The rooks any time might have swallowed ungrateful.

Caterpillars, slugs, as it grew, have counted on it,
And man the planter bent his gaze down on it fateful.

The thing will go to market, it must be picked up and loaded,
The salesman will doubt it or chuck it anyway in,
A horse must be harnessed first, or a donkey goaded
Before the purchaser may ever the first price pay for it.

Who may be now trembling with a vast impatience
And anxieties and mixed hopes for a resurrection
Out of the mouldering soil – to be new form, have perfections
Of flowers and petal and blade, to die, to be born to clean
     action.[141]

If the hope for belief in a possible resurrection comes from a complex
awareness of the necessary cruelty which is life's struggle, that grim
optimism seems to be quite lacking in the sonnet's mangled thing
limper than a grocery bill. And yet it is but a different angle within
the same field of vision: the twisted bill reminds us of the fact
that human culture refines the cruel destruction of life through its
deals. The bill is, after all, a demand for goods delivered or services
rendered; the final brief summary (the bottom line) to a hugely
complex set of relations and exchanges – with all its possible cheats,
fiddles and twists which lead not only back down, ultimately to
the harrowing plough and the indignant toad, but simultaneously
upward to the full stomach and poetry. Survival. So the sonnet is
utterly controlled in its realization of the 'whole' of existence: how
we live within a cruel (to persist with the word) set of inescapable
realities. That is the way life is: pay the bill however corrupt. Except
that the last line suddenly reminds us of what normal 'reality' had
made us forget: indignation.

And no history of November keeps the guy.

Guy Fawkes – that twisted thing – is an icon of all those who
sought to blow 'them' up. Instead, the losers have been brought
down by that treacherous whole of history – institutionalized power.
In its established relations of rulers and the ruled are created the
conditions which kill men who believed – if only briefly – that
they were struggling for a better world; a 'land fit for heroes'.
The guy becomes the soldiers and yet the line is ambiguous
in its assertion of what *history* has become. At first it might
appear that the instability of the verb 'keep' is a source of

contradiction: is the guy subject or object? But perhaps we should think instead past November: it means, of course, that month in which the war ended. Yet, if the guy is a symbol of defeated indignation, the ironic truth of November stands for quite the opposite; peace and reconciliation. We remember the dead but in sorrow. And we do not in Remembrance turn our attention to the resentment or fierce indignation of the survivors standing about us. So the line seems finally to cancel the struggle: November does not 'keep' – hold, preserve, nurture, have faith in – the guy. On the other hand, the guy as subject then refuses to acknowledge November as the moment of peace: an act of indignation will not accept the ideal of 'Remembering' the dead in order to forget the living. And now we can add the obvious further dimension – namely November's longer historical association with Guy Fawkes and his place in the collective consciousness. For what does go on in the act of Remembrance? Children dress up and make bonfires. The guy is torched and fireworks – bangers – are let off all over England on the fifth of November. What is being celebrated? That Guy Fawkes failed: the bogey man is executed every year and his evil Popish plot exposed to remind us of the historic virtues we enjoy because he lost? Odd though that it is a child's night. The Opies, drawing up the 'Children's Calendar' in *The Lore and Language of Schoolchildren*, show that there is a continuity of celebration from Halloween (October 31st) through Mischief Night (November 4th) to Guy Fawkes Night. Different parts of Britain celebrate the first two but the last seems to cover the country; in effect they are all variations of the night when the child is allowed to do things normally forbidden – play with fire, make loud bangs, stay outdoors. In other words it is a celebration of anarchy, of order upturned. The guy is both reviled and celebrated: the lord of misrule. The poor twisted thing – straw effigy – provides them with the money ('A penny for the guy') which brings them the fireworks to celebrate destruction. If that is the spirit of November 5th, then the line

And no history of November keeps the guy

can be read as a festival of liberation: the word 'keeps' now ironically meaning imprisonment. The guy survives – indeed transcends – each November, because every year he is resurrected to be destroyed. But his spirit – the spirit of defiance, of rebellion against the institution (blow it up!) – is thrillingly preserved in the child's mind. The fierce indignation exists/expires within this network of ambiguities gnomically iconized with the effigy of the guy. He is both defeat and triumph. He is resurrected every year to be reviled but equally is associated with assertions of life – fire and poetry; dance and laughter – the thrill of danger. But then again the twisted thing reminds us of real men in real fires and real explosions. No history of November keeps – preserves – them. If the effigy is unenclosable – stretching back beyond the Gunpowder Plot, as the Opies observe, to some 'heathen' Hallowe'en celebration[142] – the real men, the guys of the War, are tragically trapped within memories they cannot escape while rejected within the November consciousness of their own culture: the ironic poppies of Remembrance are equally the opiates of forgetfulness. Shut him away.

XVI

It is the year's end, the winds are blasting, and I
Write to keep madness and black torture away
A little – it is a hurt to my head not to complain.[143]

The opening lines of 'December 30th' remind us that if incarceration shut away, it did not shut up. However, the fact of writing under such circumstances does not of itself impose upon us a need to attend to the verse as of value. There may be deep therapeutic qualities within the act of writing which are of value to Ivor Gurney and Ivor Gurney alone. So to try and argue for his significance from that premise would be a poor attempt to confront extremes of experience as self-important. Taking an example, 'To God', gives us the kind of writing which exists 'to keep madness and black torture away':

To God

Why have you made life so intolerable
And set me between four walls, where I am able
Not to escape meals without prayer, for that is possible
Only by annoying an attendant. And tonight a sensual
Hell has been put on me, so that all has deserted me
And I am merely crying and trembling in heart
For death, and cannot get it. And gone out is part
Of sanity. And there is dreadful hell within me.

And nothing helps. Forced meals there have been and electricity
And weakening of sanity by influence
That's dreadful to endure. And there is Orders
And I am praying for death, death, death,
And dreadful is the indrawing or out-breathing of breath
Because of the intolerable insults put on my whole soul,
Of the soul loathed, loathed, loathed of the soul.
Gone out every bright thing from my mind.
All lost that ever God himself designed.
Not half can be written of cruelty of man, on man,
Not often such evil guessed as between man and man.[144]

What can we say? This is horrible and hopelessly depressing. This
is the noise of despair and despite its formal reality as verse – tech-
nically – it can be nothing more for us than a pathetic moment
from a dreadful existence. This cannot bear the kind of attention
demanded by – say – the Hopkins 'desolation' sonnets, not necessarily because the latter are 'better' poems (more highly structured
or whatever), but because the conflict within Hopkins is indeed with
a 'real' God. Gurney's God seems to be indefinable life – life in all
its rotten treacheries and disillusionments; its betrayals and nothing
more:

> Gone out every bright thing from my mind.
> All lost that ever God himself designed.

which is horribly moving but not at the centre of the values with
which Ivor Gurney's true poetry actually presents us.

Perhaps we can simplify the matter: first let us acknowledge
that there was a poet Ivor Gurney who officially 'went mad' and
who wrote poems within the asylum. These poems are of variable
quality, but at their best they help to comprehend the sufferings of
a man who is now exiled from his home, his native soil, his friends,
his chance to work; who lived in a terrible solitude haunted and
tormented by the memories of life in Gloucester before the War and
then the exile of the trenches.

But second, if it would be false not to recognize that Gurney's
poetry indeed has at its essence extreme experiences which in the
end did him incurable damage (experiences of gas and shell-shock
not least), it would nevertheless be equally false not to recognize a
formidable resistance because of and, in spite of, such experiences.

There is a strong backbone of powerful beliefs defining his work: beliefs which focus intensely upon music and poetry, tradition, loyalty, community, work, kindness – in short beliefs in creativity and endurance. 'The Lock Keeper' was written, after all, with memory of the Somme and Ypres behind it; yet at the poem's centre is this unequivocal assertion of the mind and hand; of a particular culture which, like Edward Thomas, he was fortunate enough to know.

The nights winter netting birds in hedges;
The stalking wild-duck by down-river sedges:
The tricks of sailing; fashions of salmon-netting:
Cunning of practice, the finding, doing, the getting –
Wisdom of every various season or light –
Fish running, tide running, plant learning and bird flight.

Short cuts, and watercress beds, and all snaring touches,
Angling and line laying and wild beast brushes;
Badgers, stoats, foxes, the few snakes, care of ferrets,
Exactly known and judged of on their merits.
Bee-swarming, wasp-exterminating and bird-stuffing.

There was nothing he did not know; there was nothing,
        nothing.

Some men are best seen in the full day shine,
Some in half-light or the dark star-light fine:
But he, close in the deep chimney-corner, seen
Shadow and bright flare, saturnine and lean;
Clouded with smoke, wrapped round with cloak of
        thought,
He gave more of desert to me – more than I ought –
Who was more used to book-poring than bright life.

One had seen half-height covering the stretched sand
With purpose, insistent, creeping-up with silver band,
But dark determined, making wide on and sure.

So behind talk flowed the true spirit – to endure,
To perceive, to manage, to be skilled to excel, to
        comprehend;

A net of craft of eye, heart, kenning and hand.
Thousand-threaded tentaculous intellect
Not easy on a new thing to be wrecked –
Since cautious with ableness, and circumspect

In courage, his mind moved to a new stand,
And only with full wisdom used that hand.

Months of firelight and lamplight of night-times; before-bed
Revelations; a time of learning and little said
On my part, since the Master he was so wise –
Easy the lesson; while the grave night-winds' sighs
At window or up chimney incessant moaning
For dead daylight or for music or fishermen dead.
Dark river voice below heard and lock's overflow.[145]

Beyond each and every individual instance which gives us the
dreadful moments of defeat before life – 'God' – there are assertions of necessary value. The moments of despair - terrible and
deep, perhaps deeper than any other English poet – can neither
isolate nor overshadow their contraries. He is a difficult formidable
poet and how he continues to live with us, and we with him, has to
be pondered.

'A War poet whose right of honour cuts falsehood like a knife',[146]
he says of himself, perhaps unfortunately. One who 'perished . . .
from the merciless intensity of his spirit both in watching the forms
of things moving apace in the stream of change and in hammering
out the poetic forms for their just representation and acclamation',
concluded Blunden in 'Concerning Ivor Gurney',[147] which may get
us nearer the truth. A poet of War and at war, it would seem, inside
his own burning intensity, with his genius and its world.

War poet – his right is of nobler steel, the careful sword –
And night walker will not suffer of praise the word
From the sleepers, the custom-followers, the dead lives unstirred.

Only, who thought of England as two thousand years
Must keep of today's life the proper anger and fears:
England that was paid for by building and ploughing and tears.[148]

Fierce indignation: insisting that he is essential to the language
– imagining, from the lunatic's cell, how to celebrate the primary
forms of English life.

The Dancers

The dancers danced in a quiet meadow
It was winter, the soft light lit in clouds
Of growing morning – their feet on the firm

Hillside sounded like a baker's business
Heard from the yard of his beamy barn-grange.
One piped, and the measured irregular riddle
Of the dance ran onward in tangling threads . . .
A thing of the village, centuries old in charm.
With tunes from the earth they trod, and naturalness
Sweet like the need of pleasure of change.
For a lit room with panels gleaming
They practised this set by winter's dreaming
Of pictures as lovely as are in spring's range . . .
No candles, but the keen dew-drops shining . . .
And only the far jolly barking of the dog strange.[149]

3

My Dog and My Self:
J. R. Ackerley

The human heart – but I will not go on with that, I am dangerous on the subject.[1]

I

J. R. Ackerley: twenty-four years literary editor of *The Listener*. Into the office each working day: read, consider, accept, reject, commission. Converse with contributers; letters to the famous: Russell, Keynes, Dame Edith, E.M. Forster ('Darling Morgan . . . '), Arthur Waley etc. etc. Moments illuminating drab days? Office hours; institutionalized literature; an active, highly necessary functionary of the new patronage: B.B.C. man.

J. R. Ackerley: age twenty-seven – Private Secretary to His Highness the Maharajah Sahib of Chhokrapur.

J. R. Ackerley: age twenty-one – Prisoner of War.

J. R. Ackerley: age seventy-one – author of a scandalous posthumous memoir.

J. R. Ackerley: poet, playwright, travel writer, biographer, novelist, autobiographer, diarist.

II

Within each, or rather, within the *whole* of his works, J. R. Ackerley was the author of the world, or rather, worlds, observed and revealed in all their startling varieties – conversions of madness – which, simply, made life insist we understand anew. His anarchic revisions of existence freed the imagination, left it at

liberty to ponder our varied enslavements. His art was obsessed
by this irony. He thus was ensnared by the illusions of freedom;
the tragic desire to let language tell it all. What else is it there for?
What other purpose can it or we have?

These boys remained my friends for some years, until the
second war killed them or they disappeared into marriage.
They were what homosexuals call 'steadies', that is to say they
propped up one's mind, one could call upon their company and
comfort if available, if required – and if nothing more hopeful
offered. For valuable though they were, the belief remained that
one could do better, better, better, and so one continued to hurl
oneself into the fray. This *ignis fatuus* caused me to behave
inconsiderately to them at times, even to hurt the feelings my
genuine affection for them had aroused, and one at least had the
spirit to reprove me when I fobbed him off from an appointment
with a present of money because some more promising new
candidate had since appeared upon the scene. Another of them,
to whom in the beginning I had given bad marks, became in
the end, I suddenly perceived, the best and most understanding
friend I had ever made; a Welsh boy, gentle, kind, cheerful,
undemanding, self-effacing, always helpful, always happy to
return to me in spite of neglect, and in control (a rare thing)
of his jealous wife, I realized his value so deeply at last that
he involved my heart. His feet smelt, poor boy, some glandular
trouble, and out of politeness he preferred not to take off his
boots. He was killed in the war. . . .

As has already been indicated I was far from being the only
person engaged in these activities; there was indeed considerable
competition and as time passed I got to recognize some of my
rivals well by sight. . . . A number of my own intellectual friends
shared this taste of mine and might pop in; but it was tacitly
understood that this was not a social gathering, like a cocktail
party, but a serious occasion needing undistracted concentration,
like stalking or chess. To speak to each other would have been a
breach of etiquette; a nod or a wink might pass, then to the business in hand. . . . [A]s the years rolled by I saw these competitors
of mine growing older and older, greyer and greyer and, catching
sight of myself in the mirrors of saloon or public bars, would
perceive that the same thing was happening to me, that I was
becoming what guardsmen called an 'old pouff', and 'old twank',

and that my chance of finding the Ideal Friend was, like my hair, thinning and receding. Most of my prejudices had now fallen by the way, nothing in the human scene any longer disgusted me (how heart-rending the cry of the pervert to his sexologist: 'I want people to shit on my face, but even when I find them they are *never* my type'), dirt and disease worried me no more (though the state of my breath continued to do so for ever), I kept a stock of Blue Ointment handy for the elimination of crabs, and weathered a dose of anal clap without much fuss (anal, yes; I *assured* the young Grenadier that I was quite impenetrable, but he begged so hard to be allowed at any rate to try). I wanted nothing now but (the sad little wish) someone to love me. My last long emotional affair, in the torments and frustrations of which I wallowed for years, was with a deserter, who became frontally infected by a prostitute with the disease I have just mentioned. Confessing this to me when I was hoping to go to bed with him, he unbuttoned his flies to exhibit the proof, squeezing out the pus for my enlightenment. Twenty years earlier, I reflected, such a performance would have dished him for me for ever; now I saw it as one of the highest compliments I had ever been paid.[2]

'[H]e was a lucky man', Auden asserted in his review of the dead Ackerley's confession *My Father and Myself*.[3] Auden should know: but really it seems – for what it is worth – that 'lucky' is a trivial observation. Perhaps Auden was envious of Ackerley's casual indifference to judgements moral or aesthetic. He concludes the chapter with this calm redirection to the reader: 'Curiosity about myself has carried me somewhat further than I want to go, and to small result; however honestly we may wish to examine ourselves we can do no more than scratch the surface'.[4] The cliché belies the victory. For in *My Father and Myself* the dead man delivers into English that profound truth Baudelaire proposed in *Mon Coeur Mis à Nu*.

La franchise absolue, moyen d'originalité.[5]

Eliot understood this in his essay on Baudelaire: 'In his verse, he is now less a model to be imitated or a source to be drained than a reminder of the duty, the consecrated task, of sincerity. From a fundamental sincerity he could not deviate'.[6] In Joe Ackerley's writing we have one example of that terrible honesty Eliot admired in Baudelaire and which Baudelaire claimed as imperative.

III

'I was born in 1896 and my parents were married in 1919': the first sentence of *My Father and Myself* sets up a tone – yes – but equally it mocks any belief in vital moral logic and reminds us of the artifice of our conventions. Ackerley saw his life in its own absence of proprieties; nothing was ever really as it should be. Having got through the Great War, incarceration as a P.O.W. and the Spanish grippe, he survived to go up to Cambridge in 1919 where he read half of his degree in Law while 'idly turning over for the rest to English Literature – a subject we can all study for ourselves in our spare time without the need for academic instruction'.[7] Maybe so: but while there he wrote verse (some of which was published) and – more to the point – a three act play. It seems that pretty soon on coming down he had already become the son whose father would generously allow him to be a 'writer'. But the 'writer' is, on the other hand, accursed: he is the idler the *flâneur*, the waster. Indeed, recalling these days of indulgence (his father was allowing him £350 a year and a 'large pleasant study lined with books at the top of the house') words of purposelessness and self-contempt are evoked again and again: 'unsettled, restless, idle, self-conscious' because, of course 'I could not write'.

> The very boundlessness of his faith in me contributed, as time went on, to my anxiety. For I could not write, and if he did ask questions on his return from his office in the evenings: 'Well, old boy, what have you been doing today?' I felt ashamed and evasive, for I had done nothing; if he did *not* ask questions, I was equally worried by his silence: did he think me a 'loafer'? This . . . was one of his favourite words of contempt for idle, shiftless people, and although I don't now believe he ever applied it in his thoughts to me, I applied it in what I feared to be his thoughts to myself.[8]

'Il faut travailler, sinon par goût, au moins par désespoir, puisque, tout bien vérifié, travailler est moins ennuyeux que s'amuser'.[9] The truth of Baudelaire's observation lies all too heavily over the indolent shoulders of the young Ackerley. And yet we have something of a misrepresentation here; even as we imagine the spoiled young man lounging about his father's house we forget that the heart of it all is not indolence but purposelessness. Here was a chap, recall, who had scraped through the War, survived a University and written a play. Perhaps that was why Roger Ackerley was prepared to indulge the son. And yet even that can't explain the discontent one feels (and here is the source of Auden's irritation?) about the self-image. The play was, in the end, produced and the father was standing on his own, at the back, a proud spectator – that surely put Joe ahead of the rest. And yet not; for perhaps it is the very nature of the play which reveals the truths which in turn anticipate the bizarre life of the later posthumous work. The act of writing in a sense pretends to (but can never) master life. It may tell us truth but what is the 'good' of that? And yet here is Ackerley's characteristically matter-of-fact view: '. . . I think that life is so important and, in its workings, so upsetting that nobody should be spared, but that it should [be] rammed down their throats from morning to night. And may those that cannot take it die of it; it is what we want. Away, away with the obstructionists that clog our lives. Let us be liberated and free in our minds.'[10] Truth here begets freedom? But how? For surely it exacts a terrible toll. But then again perhaps Ackerley had it – truth – rammed down his own throat willy-nilly. And where then is freedom?

IV

Stephen Spender:

In the early Thirties when Christopher Isherwood and I used to go every summer to Sellin on the Baltic island of Ruegen, we would walk on the beach discussing writers who had become legendary to us. A figure whom we much speculated about was J. R. Ackerley, author of a play called *The Prisoners of War* (rather inaccurately so, since it was about a group of English prisoners interned in a rather comfortable *pension* in Switzerland). What intrigued us about this play was its, for that time, extraordinarily open and candid, grimly ironic, treatment of the theme of homosexuality. Questioned by the young man who is the object of his passion about his attitude to 'the fair sex,' the hero (obviously a self-portrait of the author) retorts: 'Which sex is that?' In such a fragment of dialogue a writer seems to sum up an attitude which challenges some readers to reject him, others to make him the object of a cult.[11]

Certainly when compared with a play obviously 'about' the Great
War – say *Journey's End* - *The Prisoners of War* does strike a perverse
note. If Sherriff's play presents the War on the stage in the dugout
and menacingly off beyond it, its powerful tension serves to create
the dramatic environment necessary to suggest in Stanhope a hero
of the time. Whisky keeps down the shakes and destroys memory.
Fighting funk: that is the heroic nightmare which has to be endured
in ways we have come to expect precisely because of works like
Journey's End. The power of the drama comes from its absolute
directness; its lack of alternatives creates, in fact, its ironies. As the
play ends, the action grinds remorselessly on: the war isn't over,
just this pathetic moment of a little group of harrowed men.

> [*There is quiet in the dugout for a long time.* STANHOPE *sits with
> one hand on* RALEIGH'S *arm, and Raleigh lies very still. Presently
> he speaks again – hardly above a whisper.*]
> Dennis –

STANHOPE: Yes, old boy?

RALEIGH: Could we have a light? It's – it's so frightfully dark
and cold.

STANHOPE [*rising*]: Sure! I'll bring a candle and get another blanket.

> [STANHOPE *goes to the left-hand dugout, and* RALEIGH *is alone,
> very still and quiet, on* OSBORNE'S *bed. The faint rosy glow of
> the dawn is deepening to an angry red. The grey night sky is
> dissolving, and the stars begin to go. A tiny sound comes from
> where* RALEIGH *is lying – something between a sob and a moan.*
> STANHOPE *comes back with a blanket. He takes a candle from the
> table and carries it to* RALEIGH'S *bed. He puts it on the box beside*
> RALEIGH *and speaks cheerfully.*]
> Is that better, Jimmy? [RALEIGH *make no sign.*] Jimmy –
> [*Still* RALEIGH *is quiet.* STANHOPE *gently takes his hand. There is
> a long silence.* STANHOPE *lowers* RALEIGH'S *hand to the bed, rises,
> and takes the candle to the back of the table. He sits on the bench
> behind the table with his back to the wall, and stares listlessly
> across at the boy on* OSBORNE'S *bed. The solitary candle-flame
> throws up the lines on his pale, drawn face, and the dark shadows
> under his tired eyes. The thudding of the shells rises and falls like
> an angry sea. A* PRIVATE SOLDIER *comes scrambling down the
> steps, his round, red face wet with perspiration, his chest heaving
> for breath.*]

SOLDIER: Message from Mr. Trotter, sir – will you come at once.

[STANHOPE *gazes round at the* SOLDIER – *and makes no other sign.*]

Mr. Trotter, sir – says will you come at once! [STANHOPE *rises stiffly and takes his helmet from the table.*]

STANHOPE: All right, Broughton, I'm coming.

[The SOLDIER *turns and goes away.* STANHOPE *pauses for a moment by* OSBORNE'S *bed and lightly runs his finger over* RALEIGH'S *tousled hair. He goes stiffly up the steps, his tall figure black against the dawn sky. The shelling has risen to a great fury. The solitary candle burns with a steady flame, and* RALEIGH *lies in the shadows. The whine of a shell rises to a shriek and bursts on the dugout roof. The shock stabs out the candle-flame; the timber props of the door cave slowly in, sandbags fall and block the passage to the open air. There is darkness in the dugout. Here and there the red dawn glows through the jagged holes of the broken doorway. Very faintly there comes the dull rattle of machine-guns and the fevered spatter of rifle fire.*][12]

THE PLAY ENDS

To see Raleigh dead (and buried) moves us because his sacrifice is but an instance of the whole culture of noble suffering which the play rightly loathes. What is duty? The irony of his death is, of course, rooted in his hapless infatuation with the school hero, Stanhope. The Captain of rugby and cricket is now a drunken wreck. Duty to what? Raleigh dies; Stanhope survives. But, remember, the action is not at an end. Stanhope, as it were, knows that. We share the futility; audience and character know as much as each other. His survival simply reminds us of the grander pointlessness the play forces us to acknowledge:

[OSBORNE *turns to his book. There is silence.*]

What are you reading?

OSBORNE [*wearily*]: Oh, just a book.

TROTTER: What's the title?

OSBORNE [*showing him the cover*]: Ever read it?

TROTTER [*leaning over and reading the cover*]: *Alice's Adventures in Wonderland* – why, that's a kid's book!

OSBORNE: Yes.

TROTTER: You aren't *reading* it?

OSBORNE: Yes.
TROTTER: What – a *kid*'s book.
OSBORNE: Haven't you read it?
TROTTER [*scornfully*]: No!
OSBORNE: You ought to. [*Reads*]

> How doth the little crocodile
>   Improve his shining tail,
> And pour the waters of the Nile
>   On every golden scale?
>
> How cheerfully he seems to grin
>   And neatly spread his claws,
> And welcomes little fishes in
>   With gently smiling jaws!

TROTTER [*after a moment's thought*]: I don't see no point in that.
OSBORNE [*wearily*]: Exactly. That's just the point.
TROTTER [*looking curiously at* OSBORNE]: You *are* a funny chap![13]

So, within this truth the play explores its characters' relationships. It is essential, therefore, to the central friendship that it be understood exactly as it appears: Raleigh dies pathetically within his schoolboy illusions about asexual heroes of the playing field; Stanhope's tragedy is that he's survived to become a man. But there must be no hint of any extra side to Raleigh's infatuation: his 'love' is as simple as the pointless conflict raging about him. By this touchstone, then, recalling Spender's speculations about *The Prisoners of War* and its mysterious author, Ackerley's play would indeed seem to be, in the obvious sense of the word, perverse. The following, from a letter Ackerley wrote to Spender, on the other hand, helps to set certain matters straight.

When the play was first done, 30 years ago, a few critics voiced an understandable surprise to find not barbed wire and bayonets, but comparative luxury. A title like *The Interned* would have prepared them for that, or should have, and for the introduction into the plot of characters extraneous to the central action. In fact the whole set was authentic, and when Conrad voices the opinion that he is unhappier, more unsettled, as an internee than he was in German hands he is voicing what was, in fact, the general truth. Character had already begun to disintegrate in German hands – some of the chaps had been in [prisoner of war camps] for years – and comfort, when they got it, was unacceptable to them. They felt that they should not be enjoying it; the life-and-death struggle was still going on on the Western front; they all wished to go back into it to 'do their bit'; they could no longer escape; they felt ashamed, cowards. The place offered rest and happiness; they could accept neither; the jealousies and bickerings were endless. That was the background. As for homosexuality. I'm sorry you thought that there were 'one or two' homosexual characters. If that were so it would certainly be a fault . . . There is only one homosexual character, Conrad himself. The rest are entirely normal.[14]

We can return to the question of homosexuality in a moment but first it must be made clear that part of the play's real problem is the lack of dramatic action. Unlike *Journey's End* there is no strong *fact* looming over the piece; no big raids and days to be counted off in waiting. Rather – and this seems to take us somewhere important – the very ideas of the piece are necessarily concerned with inaction, with obviously being confined, with idling about. The play, curiously, reminds us of Ackerley's contemptuous self-descriptions of life as a failed writer in his father's house. But it is important, equally, to recognize the psychological truth being got at. In his Introduction to *Escapers All* Ackerley quotes Captain J. L. Hardy's reminiscence of his brief time in enemy hands:

I felt my captivity very much more at Augustabad than in any place where I have since been. The camp was a hotel which had been converted, and the food though not too plentiful, was good, while the staff were polite and our rooms clean and comfortable. I was only in the camp for ten days, but was perfectly miserable during the whole of that time, and I do not think I was hypersensitive in that it seemed to me abominable that I should be leading a life of comfort at such a time. It was never again my lot to find myself in a good camp, and of that I am glad . . . .[15]

About which Ackerley has this to say:

So you see that the urge to escape sprang from something much deeper than physical conditions; it sprang from a very deep human instinct indeed – the need for self-expression; and that is why these stories must appeal to all of us, for they touch a universal note which inspires our own actions, not only in war but in peace. Prisoners of war were on the shelf, and they felt it all the time. They were unimportant, they were unused, and especially to educated men that is a very dreadful thing indeed. It was not just being separated from countries, families, friends; it was not just being out of the war; it went deeper than that; it was a thwarting of the free and natural growth of individual life, and it has permanently stunted many a once eager and ambitious spirit.[16]

And he would know:

Ackerley, J. R. Captain 8th East Surrey Regiment. Joined up in October 1914 at the age of 17. Wounded on the Somme July 1st, 1916. Again wounded and taken prisoner in May 1917. Spent eight months in Germany, first in the hospital in Hanover, then at prison-camps of Karlsruhe, Heidelberg and Augustabad. Invalided to Switzerland, where he was interned for the rest of the war.[17]

This is the biography offered at the beginning of *Escapers All*. So Ackerley had lived through Sherriff's play; had been taken out on the first day of the Somme. To that we shall come in a moment; but first exactly what he is telling us, in this introduction, about his perverse drama of inaction should now be made clear.

The passage continues:

They are not by any means typical [escapers]; they are very rare, for the vast majority of prisoners, I think, tried to find other means of escape – tried, that is to say, to preserve the balance and fitness of their minds in other ways: in writing, or reading, or friendships, or learning languages, or by taking up the various other pursuits and sports that their circumstances offered.[18]

Which makes it sound very familiar indeed – imprisoned in an isolated country house, forced by that circumstance to do things:

take up sports, learn stuff, make friends – this, surely, is the average English middle-class public school-boy's mandatory passage towards manhood. Above all, in making friends. But, of course, that is a word about which English middle-class public school-boys must be careful. Nonetheless, to a degree, *The Prisoners of War* can be read within the constraints suggested by *Journey's End* – adolescent emotions are explored in their unwilling projection beyond adolescent realities. In *The Prisoners of War*, however, the madness of real life – real imprisonment, real isolation – is, unlike *Journey's End*, with its inconclusive fire-storm, climactic but insignificant death, uttered in a dramatic undertone. And, of course, it is within the limbo, precisely within the apparently timeless wasting away of lives, in the climaxless inaction of internment, that the differences between Ackerley's drama and 'normal' war literature can flourish. It's all about differences.

ADELBY. May I borrow this?
CONRAD [*preoccupied*]. What is it?
ADELBY. Plutarch's 'Lives.'
CONRAD. If you like. I'd sooner you took some other book.
ADELBY. What can you spare?
CONRAD. O take it; take it. It doesn't matter. [*He gets up, walks up the room, returns, and sits down again in the same seat.*]
ADELBY. I've read bits of it before. When I was a boy I used to be so stirred, I remember, by some of the tales of the heroes. The Theban band! I used to cry, too – I suppose because they were such fine heroic figures, and I [*he smiles*] – wasn't. It's a pity we've lost all that, that great hero-worship. Each man used to take his intimate friend to war with him, didn't he? And they'd protect each other. It gave a man something *real* to fight for. [*There is a pause.*]
CONRAD. Er . . . yes. [*He gets up again and crosses to the door, stepping nervously on the patterns of the carpet.*] Adelby – what's the matter with me? [*He returns to his chair, stepping carefully on the patterns, but does not sit down.*]
ADELBY. [*his chair held grotesquely under one arm*]. I believe it's what clever people call your 'ego.' [*He blinks at him amiably.*]
CONRAD. [*returning to the door, spelling out the syllables on the carpet as he goes*]. My e-go. I suppose that means I'm too selfish?
ADELBY [*putting his chair down and sitting on it*]. Er, no, it doesn't.
CONRAD. *Am* I too selfish?

ADELBY. Well – introspective, repressed.
CONRAD [*on the march again*]. Yes, I am. [*Pause.*] I suppose. [ADELBY,
    puffing at his pipe, contemplates him gravely.] But that's rela-
    tive. There's no one who shares me, frees me, takes me out
    of myself. There never has been.
        . . .
    Is all this of any use – in *any* case? You see – you don't
    quite understand. I'm – I think I'm – different.
ADELBY. Like everyone else, Jim. That's what I meant by your
    ego. But don't be unhappy about it. It's such waste – to
    be unhappy.
CONRAD [*abruptly*]. How old are you?
ADELBY. Thirty-eight.
CONRAD. Yes. [*He continues his march.*] Then I'm a hundred. [*Silence.*]
    Do *you* look upon yourself as being a very complicated
    piece of mechanism?
ADELBY. I used to.
CONRAD. I suppose you're more or less settled down? You under-
    stand yourself now?
ADELBY. I don't think I shall ever astonish myself again.
CONRAD. Are you very happy?
ADELBY. Underneath all this fret – yes.
CONRAD. You haven't always been?
ADELBY [*disturbed*]. No. No, I haven't. But that's – over. I shall
    never be unhappy again. I'd – I'd throw my life away rather
    than be unhappy again.[19]

'You see – you don't quite understand. I'm – I think – I'm –
different'. With which Adelby rightly – and wrongly – disagrees
since we're all different. Yes but there is different and there is
different. And for Ackerley that difference is intimately bound up
within friendship and, eventually, love. So Conrad attempts to get
through to Adelby again: here's someone else who's 'different':

CONRAD. Would you? I get very tired of life sometimes. [*Pause.*] Are
    we, any of us, as complicated as we think we are, I wonder.
    Do you think religion helps a man?
ADELBY [*trying to follow*]. Religion, Jim?
CONRAD. Abstract beliefs, or – idols, you know. Mere symbols?
ADELBY. I don't know, Jim. A man's own religion helps him
    sometimes, I suppose; but no one else's – unless it hap-
    pens to fit.

CONRAD. Yes, that's it – 'unless it happens to fit.' When I was interned in Germany I met an officer who loved a rabbit. He'd bought it for twelve marks. There was nothing else in his life. [*Whimsically*] He used to read short stories to it out of a magazine. [*Abruptly*] Poor devil! He was mad, of course. [*Pause. Very low*] But he was happy. [*Getting lost*] I was happy then, too. In a way. I almost wish I was back.[20]

It is the pressure on the increasingly isolated Conrad which creates the dramatic action.

He seeks 'friendship' in the shape of young Grayle. Instead his attempts at creating a camerado are boorishly rebuffed. Ackerley successfully increases Conrad's sense of isolated bitterness by introducing an ironically asexual 'normal' friendship between two other prisoners. The homosexual Conrad is humiliatingly crippled by his emotions: by the end of Act Two (the play is in three acts), in a fit of wounded jealous pride, he lays one on the object of desire, hitting him heavily in the mouth. Ackerley skilfully clouds the motives for the attack: desire and jealousy are seethingly at one with his growing isolation and despair so that the blow is as much against the very fact of emotions and feelings in general as against the particular human being. Sexuality is a curse. The play's *dénouement* is contrived but neatly enough not to irritate. Conrad hands Adelby ('I shall never be unhappy again. I'd – I'd throw my life away rather than be unhappy again') the telegram which informs of his wife's death from the grippe; Adelby throws himself off a mountain; Conrad has a fit and is left in a state of shock. The doubling-up of the different 'love' stories (you can't win either way: life is unhappy because love is spurned; life is unhappy because true companionship is destroyed) manages both to accent differences and eliminate them. Conrad's insanity, however, does stray into new realms of the bizarre. His direct response to the varied destructions of love is as much an articulation of public virtue – loyalty to a comrade – as, it would seem, an emotional response to the cruelties of existence whether Adelby's or his own:

We're no use to anyone. Why should anyone take trouble over us? I suppose half the world thinks of us as pariahs, outsiders, cowards – if it thinks of us at all.[21]

This works well within the No Man's Land between self-pity and truth. Here the weird are not in fact a prima facie subculture: all the prisoners (married or bachelor, homosexual, whatever) are outcasts. All men in this war are made to seem, as Adelby had observed, 'different'. You would rather get back and be killed than pointlessly drift about in the hotel. But then you'd rather not get out and face the fate of Raleigh – say – in *Journey's End*. In Ackerley's play life becomes endless pointless moments with men trying to find a means of mental escape, 'to preserve the balance and fitness of their minds in other ways'.[22] So, in the end, Conrad emulates his fellow-officer; the man who loved his rabbit:

> I've got a plant to look after now. [*He waves his hand towards it.*] Can't be bothered with anything else. Plants or rabbits; it's the same thing.[23]

And just what are we to make of all this? On immediate reflection Conrad's perverseness seems a perversely perverse end to the play's complex moral action: to have manoeuvered him from the alienation of his normally 'perverse' sexual desires towards a total emotional imprisonment which can find escape only within the love for a plant would appear, all things considered, to offer a whimsically bizarre dramatic twist. We are all different. Exactly so and thus the final difference is necessary to show just how really different difference has to be. And yet, we should remind ourselves, the play is based upon a perverse premise in the first instance: the prisoners must strive to achieve illness if they are to be released. The healthier you are the more a prisoner: as the body flourishes so the spirit withers. And then again, within the genre of 'War Books', perversely two of the central characters are women: the matronly Mrs. Prendergast, organizer of the officer's dance and, more cunningly, the sexually dominant Mme Louis, the loutish Grayle's successful seducer and thus a constituent cause of Conrad's alienation and equally, to return to the beginning, his transcendence of it.

The triumph of perverseness – nothing is what it seems or should be. Everything generates its contradiction: that is the deep thematic constant of Ackerley's life and work. Just as his own perverse existence – imprisoned within the miserable unsatisfied promiscuous pursuit of the 'Ideal Friend' – is perversely transformed by the love of and for the female, so all of our certainties about the nature of moral judgement are continuously confounded. There is no life without love since love promises to cheat imprisonment and, in its turn, becomes itself a cheat. Life thus is inescapably ironic – we exist within realms neither tragic nor comic by turns but simultaneously so. In its way, Ackerley's art creates the consciousness of the hastening reveller and the mourning friend.

So it is important to note, not just for the sake of the play itself, but for the illumination of the dark sources of Ackerley's work, one more instance of the perverse, namely that in *The Prisoners of War* (as Spender noted) we have, unlike *Journey's End*, *qua* war no war. What was Ackerley avoiding? For The *Prisoners of War* is as much an act of omission as it is of confession. Not only are Ackerley's own dreadful experiences of the War obliterated but, equally, memories of an older brother and his fate at the Front are also absent. The final perverse truth of the play is that it was written to repress truths of another kind. And, having therein succeeded, Ackerley spent the rest of his life struggling to find ways of confessing the lie: this is, of course, the ultimate paradox of the truth-teller.

IV

The significance of the missing brother cannot be underestimated. He appears in *My Father and Myself* as yet another of the parents' seemingly casual accommodations to existence.

My elder brother Peter was the accident. 'Your father happened to have run out of french letters that day,' remarked my Aunt Bunny with her Saloon Bar laugh, and I have for some time been aware that if I am to get this history even approximately straight I must somehow steer a course between my aunt's rabelaisian humour, my mother's romanticism, and the mutual jealousies of both. Nevertheless my brother was neither intended nor wanted and efforts, probably of an amateur kind, were made to prevent his arrival. My mother was thirty-one years old at this time and working on the stage, a more respectable stage than the one Aunt Bunny was to reach, known indeed as the 'legitimate' stage (she was a recruit of Sir Herbert Beerbohm Tree): this is not however to suggest that she should therefore have known better. Doctors

were confidentially consulted, various homely remedies pre-
scribed, and all manner of purges, nostrums, and bodily exercises
employed to bring about a miscarriage. But my brother was not
to be quenched. Nevertheless he did not survive unscathed. He
emerged prematurely, double-ruptured, jaundiced and black in
the face, presenting altogether so wretched and puny an appearance with his head sunk between his shoulders like a tortoise that
the doctor in attendance remarked, more prophetically, it may be
thought, than he realized, 'Seems hardly worth saving.'[24]

Even so the father came to favour the oldest son: for he became in
time very much himself;

Fed at first through a quill, for he could not suck, and wrapped
in cotton wool soaked in cod-liver oil, this flickering life was
gradually brought, mainly by the unremitting care and skill
of my grandmother, through a sickly childhood, to become
in time a tall, thin, dark, rather sallow youth of a lively and
good-tempered disposition. He liked practical jokes and all forms
of buffoonery, was good at playing cricket and the bones, had a
charming natural tenor voice and a leaning towards the stage:
he collected pictures of Henry Irving and Beerbohm Tree and
was always acting and dressing up. This was in my mother's
tradition, but the paternal influence was stronger and he was
training to enter our father's business when the 1914 war broke
out. This brought in the paternal example again: my mother
said, 'Thank Heaven my boys are too young to join up', and
we offered ourselves to the Army at once. I was accepted; my
brother, who had been obliged to wear a truss throughout his life,
was rejected.[25]

He approximated far closer to the paternal image, a chip off the
old block destined to fulfil his father's cherished ambitions: marriage and children and the family business, that was to be Peter's
lot. On the other hand 'he would not have written this book':[26] an
eery observation in the light of what was to come. Above all, like
his military parent and unlike, apparently, his younger brother, he
was tough. The apple of the father's eye:

From sculling on the river at Richmond where we lived, my

brother developed blisters on the palm of one hand, and my father, in whom the original guardsman persisted, told him that the best way to harden blisters was to rub one's own urine into them. This barrack-room remedy resulted in a badly poisoned hand, the whole of the palm oozed with pus. Dr. Wadd was summoned and said, 'You can bear a spot of pain, Pete old lad, can't you, or do you want an anaesthetic?' I myself would firmly have demanded an anaesthetic, total if possible, local (if invented then) at least, whatever the expression on my father's face might have been, but my brother said, 'Go ahead'. Wadd then borrowed a pair of scissors from my mother and slit the whole puffed-up palm across. My brother did utter a gasp, turned green and almost fainted; but it was what my father would have called a 'jolly good show'.[27]

Yet, all things considered, the relationship between the brothers was obviously a good one: unlikes were able to develop in their own spaces:

He was smoking one of my father's Gentleman cigars and wearing an Edward VII grey felt hat, a heavy reddish-purple overcoat with a belt, patent leather shoes and a monocle. He carried a slender cane like Charlie Chaplin and was beginning to spot round the mouth. I thought he looked an awful ass and rather a cad; not of course foreseeing that in a few years' time I myself might be sighted in London dressed in a voluminous black carabiniero's cloak, cast over one shoulder in the Byronic manner, and trailed by children calling out rude remarks.

After that I remember nothing more about my brother until our last melodramatic meeting. This was in a dug-out in France, in a ditch called the Boom Ravine.[28]

This last melodramatic meeting is central to the perverse nature of *The Prisoners of War*. Of course it takes us out beyond theatrical walls into the trenches and death. The account of active service – apart from a brief digression in *Hindoo Holiday* – is confined to one chapter of *My Father and Myself*. It is a confinement which deals, perhaps, both with expression *and* repression as if only within his posthumous work could the terrible facts and feelings of these experiences be uttered. Because the truth is terrible: a nightmare which he obviously sought to escape throughout his life.

V

The first day of the Somme:

These wounds of mine are not without interest, at any rate to me.
They showed me something which I was to notice often again in
my character, that I have a fairly well-developed instinct for self-
preservation, both physical and moral. If the old campaigner of
Tel-el-Kebir [i.e. Ackerley's father] had known as much about my
wounds as I did, what would he have thought of me? The Battle
of the Somme, Sir Douglas Haig's masterly operation, has often
been described. This vast, full-scale attack was prepared for by
an incessant bombardment of the German lines, prolonged over
many days and so heavy that, we were told, all resistance would
be crushed, the enemy wire destroyed, their trenches flattened,
and such Germans as survived reduced to a state of gibbering
imbecility. It would be, for us, a walk-over. Very different was
our reception. The air, when we at last went over the top in
broad daylight, positively hummed, buzzed, and whined with
what sounded like hordes of wasps and hornets but were, of
course, bullets. Far from being crushed, the Germans were in
full possession of senses better than our own; their smartest
snipers and machinegunners were coolly waiting for us. G.H.Q.,
as was afterwards realized, had handed the battle to them by
snobbishly distinguishing us officers from the men, giving us
revolvers instead of rifles and marking our rank plainly upon
our cuffs. The 'gibbering imbeciles' confronting us were thus
enabled to pick off the officers first, which they had been carefully
instructed to do, leaving our army almost without leadership.

Many of the officers in my battalion were struck down the
moment they emerged into view. My company commander was
shot through the heart before he had advanced a step. Neville (*sic*),
the battalion buffoon, who had a football for his men to dribble
over to the 'flattened and deserted' German lines and was then
going to finish off any 'gibbering imbecile' he might meet with
the shock of his famous grin (he had loose dentures and could
make a skull-like grimace when he smiled), was also instantly
killed, and so was fat Bobby Soames, my best friend.[29] I had spent
the previous evening with him and he had said to me quietly,
without emotion, 'I'm going to be killed tomorrow. I don't know
how I know it but I do.' How far I myself got I don't remember;

not more than a couple of hundred yards is my guess. I flew over the top like a greyhound and dashed forward through the wasps, bent double. Squeamish always about blood, mutilations and death, averting my gaze, so far as I could, from the litter of corpses left lying about whenever we marched up to the line through other regiments' battle-fields, never hurrying when word was passed down to me, as duty officer in the trenches, that someone had been killed or wounded, in the hope that, if I dawdled, the worst of the mess might be cleared up before I arrived, my special private terror was a bullet in the balls, which accounts psychologically, for it was, of course, unavailing physically, for the crouched up attitude in which I hurled myself at the enemy. The realization that I was making an ass of myself soon dawned; looking back I saw that my platoon was still scrambling out of the trench, and had to wait until they caught up with me. My young Norfolk servant, Willimot, who then walked at my side, fell to the ground. 'I'm paralysed, sir,' he whimpered, his face paper-white, his large blue ox-like eyes terrified. A bullet, perhaps aimed at me with my revolver and badges, had severed his spine. My platoon-sergeant, Griffin, lifted him into a shell-hole and left him there. Then I felt a smack on my left upper arm. Looking down I saw a hole in the sleeve and felt the trickling of blood. Then my cap flew off. I picked it up and put it on again; there was a hole in the crown. Then there was an explosion in my side, which sent me reeling to the ground. I lay there motionless. Griffin and one of the men picked me up and put me in a deep shell-hole. Griffin then tried to unbutton my tunic to examine and perhaps dress my wound. I was not unconscious, only dazed, and I had by now a notion of what had happened. It was another instance of the credulity of the time – my company commander's contribution – that we officers had been told to carry a bottle of whisky or rum in our haversacks for the celebration of our victory after the 'walk-over'. Some missile had struck my bottle of whisky and it had exploded. Of this I became dimly aware when Sergeant Griffin moved me; I felt the crunch of broken glass in the sack beneath my arm. What precisely had occurred I did not know; besides the smarting that had now started in my arm I had a sensation of smarting in my side, so I was damaged there also, though by what or how much I could not tell. What I do remember perfectly well is resisting Griffin's attempts to examine me. I lay with my eyes closed and

my wounded arm clamped firmly to my wounded side so that
he could not explore beneath my tunic. I did not want to know,
and I did not want *him* to know, what had happened to me. I did
not feel ill, only frightened and dazed. I could easily have got
up, and if I could have got up I should have got up. But I was
down and down I stayed. Though my thoughts did not formulate
themselves so clearly or so crudely at the time, I had a 'Blighty'
one, that sort of wound that all the soldiers sighed and sang for
('Take me back to dear old Blighty'), and my platoon, in which I
had taken much pride, could now look after itself.

My injuries were indeed of a shamefully trivial nature; a bullet
had gone through the flesh of my upper arm, missing the bone,
and a piece of shrapnel or bottle glass (I can't remember which)
had lodged beneath the skin of my side above the ribs. The
explosion must therefore have been fairly violent to have driven
this object through my tunic and shirt. I was welcomed home like
a conquering hero and was disinclined to exhibit my wounds
when requested by sympathetic admirers to do so, though not
disinclined to give the impression that the exploding bottle had
entirely deprived me of my senses. Yet so strange are we in our
inconsistencies that I was not happy in Blighty and, in a few
months' time, got myself sent back to France. I was at once
promoted to the rank of captain. Soon afterwards my brother
joined me.[30]

How does one recover – in mind, in spirit – from such an experience? Ackerley (like Graves and Sassoon among others) returned as
soon as possible; but what is it in the return? Something perhaps to
do with guilt? For surely modesty isn't really an end in itself when
he describes the wound as of 'a shamefully trivial nature'. It *was*
a Blighty; one that soldiers sighed and sang for. Something then,
which couldn't be assuaged, corrupts the memory so that promotion
has to be played down, shrugged aside, received unworthily.

To be alive, part of the 'race apart' yet apart; clearly no spirit can
be at peace when others are still out there or are dead.

VII

Now healed, Captain Ackerley found himself on the line while his
older but subordinate brother (still a Lieutenant) was in a reserve

company behind. All he can later see of their coming together is the 'last meeting': memory evidently exists to repress all that can be held down but – alas – the last meeting cannot, will not, go away. Called up to the line, Second Lieut. Peter Ackerley is given the opportunity to lead his men in a 'stunt' – a common or garden suicide mission involving a tiresome German salient from which fire could be thrown down upon the British trenches: the force was to shove off from Captain Ackerley's position in the front line. And now the real drama plays itself out. First the details backstage; the jaunty Lieutenant arrives late; his watch has stopped; his men are slack, even undisciplined; he casually swaps watches with Joe; refuses a drink ('I'll take my rum with the men') and finally makes the farewell:

> Then my brother's hand thrust out to shake my own, his twisty smile, my 'Good luck', his jocular salute. 'Don't worry, sir', said he to the Major as he left. It was his only piece of self-indulgence. His thin putteed legs retreated up the dugout steps and the sack curtain swung to behind him. I never saw him again.[31]

And so Joe watched; living and simultaneously burying it all. The narrative's 'I don't knows', I 'can't be sures', are a kind of hopeless release from the ghastly details as the night rolls on and the older Lieutenant fails to return:

> I have some recollection still of the place from which I watched my brother's start. It was a shattered and abandoned gun-emplacement in the ravine, which I had used for observation purposes before. It offered an extensive view of the German lines and of Point 85. My manuscript says that my orderly went with me; maybe he did, orderlies were almost permanent attachments, but I remember nothing about him; I expect that I myself, my feelings and sensations, occupied the forefront of my thought. I dimly recall scrambling up the steep earthy slope of this advanced post and lying there beneath the broken beams of its roof, my head cautiously raised above the level of the ground. Time no longer exists; how long I remained there I haven't a notion. But I recollect, as in a dream, an inferno scene suddenly opening, whistlings, shouts, rifle and machine-gun fire, advancing figures momentarily illuminated by the flash

of bursting shells and the firework flares of Very lights against
a background of drifting smoke, and a bunch of three or four
men, curiously attitudinized, near the German trenches – then
bullets struck the ground around me and one sent up a spurt
of earth against my cheek. That I remember well, that little spurt
of earth against my cheek. Soon afterwards shells began to whizz
over and crump in the ravine behind. Retaliation had begun and
I made my way back to the dugout.

Then nothing but the slow dragging of time, the racket, the
flames of the candles dipping and blinking as the Boom Ravine
began to boom, the occasional cascades of earth and stones that
came rattling down the dugout steps from the exploding world
above. The field telephone rang from time to time, the Colonel
wanted news, the Brigadier was getting impatient; if the Major
was resting, as he mostly was, lying on his back on a wire bunk,
his hands clasped behind his head, I took the calls for him.
Then – how much later? – a stumbling on the steps and one of
my brother's men appeared, a smear of blood upon his face, to
say he had got lost, was wounded in the hand; and the Major
sitting up in bed and suddenly taking charge, his cold, cutting
questions, his demand for the fellow's name and number, his
orders to him to return instantly to his unit or he would have
him court-martialled and shot for desertion. No soldier might
fall out, he said, unless he was dead or too crippled to walk. Did
I remember then my own performance on 1 July or had it not yet
reached the cold, clear light of objective self-criticism?[32]

Thus his brother was lying wounded out there in No Man's
Land, 'and might have been the merest litter left about after a
riotous party, for all the interest the Brigadier, the Colonel or the
Major evinced in his fate. And I did nothing either'.[33] Of course
Ackerley himself had been there before – on July 1st 1916 – and
was to be there again. But this was his own brother: his genes were
out there.

If their life's blood drained out of them meanwhile that was
hard luck; one did not risk other lives to seek them out and
bring them in. Or one's own . . . . Officially again, the matter had
nothing to do with me; such exalted persons as myself did not
crawl out into no man's land to bring in the wounded, and if this
particular officer had been the comparative stranger he should

have been I would probably have had a nap like the Major. But he was not a stranger, and though my conscience managed in the ensuing years to blot out the details of the event, it remained for so long in my mind as an uneasiness that it must have seemed to me at the time that life was once again making upon me one of those monstrous and unfair demands with which I could not cope, that I was being put to another unwelcome test.

How long did this disgusting situation continue?[34]

'This disgusting situation' – indeed what more can one say. The safe brother is tormented, conscience-wracked – and utterly impotent. With the Major, a game of moral cat and mouse is played out; one which certainly must have added its layer of self-contempt as years later Ackerley brooded over the manuscript from which he had to rewrite and retrieve these events – events which are unmentioned in his own life-time; events which he can only publish when it no longer matters:

How long did this disgusting situation continue? It certainly worsened. My manuscript says that retaliation slackened and ceased and that a message came from my duty officer, Dyson, to say that my brother had managed to crawl back to within fifty yards of the front line and should he send out men to bring him in? It says I went out and climbed on to the roof of the dugout – a courageous act? – to look about. Dawn was breaking, the enemy lines were clearly visible. It says I returned to the dugout, where the Major was now sitting at a table writing his report, and said to him, 'I don't think it's safe to send out men to bring my brother in, do you? It's rather light,' and the brute replied, 'You have seen how light it is. Do as you think fit.' A painfully convincing piece of dialogue and not at all what I wanted. But it seems I got that in the end, for my manuscript adds that I then said, 'I think I'll go along and see Dyson myself,' and the Major replied, 'I want you here.' My answer to Dyson's message is not noted and lies beyond recall; it may have been that no one should go out to bring my brother in until further orders.

I sometimes wondered in after years about the Major, that strange enigmatic man, what he meant, what he felt, what he guessed or knew. Had he turned his back upon me on purpose, to leave me free to deal with my personal problems as I wished and in spite of his directives?[35]

The 'other' is certainly necessary for the moral torment: surely to disobey here is the point of heroism. But Ackerley is trapped; convinced of his own failure, of the rabbit within. There were precedents for disobedience – the Thorne brothers, subalterns in the battalion: one had failed to return and the other 'who adored him' strode out and 'in defiance of orders, . . . brought his dead body in slung over his shoulder, walking heavily back in the early dawn'.[36] But you could always be tried and shot.

Guilt then; guilt inescapable and all-engulfing. For at the front no one is outside, no one is objective. Even as Ackerley pondered the Major's apparent indifference – 'that strange enigmatic man' – he knew that the next time it could be *him*:

> It would have been interesting to have had, perhaps at a post-war reunion dinner over a bottle of wine, his version of it all, but he was killed soon afterwards in the Schwaben Redoubt, a colonel then, defending an indefensible position, covering with the exhausted remnant of his command his brigade's retreat, fighting hand to hand with a bayonet against overwhelming odds, encouraging his men with his personal example to the last.[37]

But the brother survived; survived to be carried in apologizing and begging to be let off the stretcher just for one more go. Why then, those many years later, did Ackerley find it necessary to go over the incident again? That he had failed? Funked it? Betrayed the brother and yet by great good fortune was not guilty? But then again – as with the Major – no man in this race of men apart is apart: judge not even yourself. Two months later, Ackerley had to take his own boys over the top: this time a different kind of luck held. As his men crouched in their shell holes awaiting reinforcements,

> . . . the Germans counter-attacked in considerable strength, firing from the hip as they advanced. The very sight of them was enough for my company. Rising as one man they deserted me and bolted. I bolted after, shouting 'Stop!' – not that I wanted them to. The vain word may well have taken on a shriller note when a bullet struck me in the bottom, splintering my pelvis, as was discovered later, and dealing me a wound where, my father had sometimes remarked, echoing Siward, no good soldier should bear one. With a flying leap that Nureyev might have envied I

landed in a shell-hole which already contained one of the things I most detested, a corpse, and was soon to harbour another wounded officer named Facer, and a man bleeding to death of a stomach wound. When dusk fell upon that foolish and revolting day I was taken prisoner. Limping off into captivity, at bayonet point and parched with thirst, I picked up from the equipment of dead men bottle after bottle, hoping for a cooling drink of water; they all contained neat rum. I was reported 'Missing', with no further news for several weeks. 'I'm not much given to praying, old chap,' wrote my brother later, 'but I don't mind telling you that I often went down on my knees and prayed to God for your safety.'[38]

He was taken prisoner and after eight months spent not uncomfortably in various prison camps in Germany, was sent, by his father's manipulations, as an intern to Switzerland. This takes us back to *The Prisoners of War*: back to the nervy tension of Conrad's desperate attempt to find escape through, or at least into, some kind of relationship. But that isn't quite all. The brother, he too went back to the battalion and became 'increasingly fed up, poor fellow, with the war he had once thought so glamorous'.[39] He was back in that other play – *Journey's End* – from which there was escape only through injury or death, where the Stanhopes were sozzling themselves to forget the truth, killing the past and future, trapped within the present. And so Joe made the unforgivable mistake of reaching out from the one play into the other, of reminding his brother that (to recall the lines from the Introduction to *Escapers All*) there was another kind of suffering in not only feeling out of the war (and hence guilty) but also in being thwarted of 'the free and natural growth of individual life'. This 'moan' when directed to the man at the front brought a swift and uncharitable response. For even though you might think you ought to 'want' to get back there presumably nobody, nobody even in his wrong mind, actually wanted it. Desire was a function of emotional trauma – guilt, shame, fear of being afraid: these were the animating forces that crippled men's minds. And so '[e]xasperated by my grousing letters and doubtless now unnerved by endless trench warfare, my brother wrote roughly to shut me up; I should consider myself bloody lucky, said he, to be where I was, and he only wished they were there too. On 7 August 1918, just before the end of hostilities, as he was filling his pipe in the trenches and turning round to hail a friend, a whizz-bang decapitated him. My

father, I am told, was profoundly shaken by a grief he was too proud
to share. Soon after the stupid war ended and I was repatriated'.[40]
This death – the experience around this death – is what has to be
repressed. And it is that guilt – for surely nothing can be done (the
father's grief is unshared) – which perversely forces the play *The
Prisoners of War* onto the page. The drama's inaction exists only
through a repression of all the war's dreadful acts. And thus it
must have curiously bonded father and son – (although what are
we to make of the paternal 'manipulation' which kept Joe out of
the war in Switzerland?) – in all manner of unstated emotional
ties. It certainly meant on the father's side (one imagines) the
toleration of his son's writing. And it must have meant on
the son's side an increasing feeling of isolation and imprisonment – guilt – which ultimately he sought to overcome through
an endless sequence of brief sexual encounters in search of the
ideal man (perhaps the ideal brother), to be retrieved through
other masculine bodies. But it never worked. All important life
was in the struggle against imprisonment and that may have been
the real difference between father and son: as was indeed suddenly
revealed. Old Roger had sought and achieved his escape (from what
though?) in a manner very much his own: a 'secret orchard'.

'For many years I had a mistress and she presented me with twin
girls ten years ago and another girl eight years ago'.[41]

Or was it? Are we not – necessarily – imprisoned within secrets?
But then Old Roger obviously regarded most of life's conventional
arrangements – above all those which ordained and regularized
sex – as being floutable. In the curiously Western struggle between
passion and society Roger was passion's man if not slave. At the
very heart of his life were its secrets.

VIII

The first question which the son had to ponder when struggling
with this elusive parent, was how exactly it came about that an
ex-guardsman could become a director of Elders and Fyffes, the
acknowledged 'Banana King', man of affairs –

It is necessary to know about my father that he had been a

guardsman. He was born on 1 April 1863, the seventh of a large family of three boys and five girls, in Prospect Cottage, Rainhill, a village near Liverpool. His father, who described himself as a share-broker, came a financial cropper in 1875 and had to remove his family to a smaller cottage nearby and send the children out to work. The girls took jobs as teachers, the boys were put to trades, my father left school at the age of thirteen and went as clerk to a firm of auctioneers in Liverpool. His schooling therefore was of the briefest.[42]

He became a strikingly handsome young man who, at the age of sixteen, ran away to London and joined the army:

The Household Cavalry are a fine body of men, much admired for their magnificent physique and the splendour of their accoutrements, but it will hardly be claimed for them that they are – or at any rate were – refined in their tastes and habits. Conscription and improved rates of pay may have brought some alteration to the scene, but in my father's young days and on into my own, sex and beer and the constant problem of how to obtain these two luxuries in anything like satisfactory measure on almost invisible means – in his day the Queen's shilling – represented the main leisure preoccupation of many guardsmen and troopers. Nor is this surprising. Healthy and vigorous young men, often, like my father, the merest boys, suddenly transplanted from a comparatively humdrum provincial or country life into a London barrack-room, exercised and trained all day to the bursting point of physical fitness, and let loose in the evening, with little money and large appetites, to prowl about the Monkey Walk in Hyde Park, the pubs, or West End streets, in uniforms of the most conspicuous and sometime provocative design – it is hardly surprising that their education in the seductions and pleasures of the world should take rapid strides. The tall handsome youth from the village of Rainhill seated with drawn sword upon his charger in Whitehall, arrayed in plumed helmet, glittering cuirass and white buckskin breeches, and gaped at by admiring spectators who sometimes dropped coins into his highly polished top boots, certainly found life very much to his taste. Unhappily my knowledge of that life and of the years that followed is meagre.

At his final discharge he brought away a good conduct badge, a second-class certificate of education, and the War Medal

and Bronze Star of the Egyptian Campaign. He brought away
two other things, the seeds of success in life and the seeds
of death . . . . So far as the former is concerned, something
has to be found to account for the transformation of Trooper
Alfred Ackerley with his second-class certificate of education
and impecunious family background in 1884, into the cultivated,
urbane, travelled and polished young man of the world with
£2,000 a year who picked up my mother on a Channel boat in
1892 and was later to become one of the directors of Elders and
Fyffes, fruit merchants, earning £12,000 a year and the title of
Banana King when he died.[43]

The answer lies, apparently, 'with two wealthy gentlemen whom
my father met in London during his five years of soldiering'.[44]
Wealthy gentlemen with an eye, we soon realize, for 'healthy and
vigorous young men . . . let loose in the evening, with little money
and large appetites, to prowl about the Monkey Walk in Hyde Park,
the pubs or West streets, in uniforms of the most conspicuous and
sometimes provocative designs. . .' Young Roger knew what he
had, knew what they wanted, and asked the price. The first was
a barrister who, indifferent to his own wife and children, took Roger
Ackerley on as a secretary and just before the young guardsman
left for the campaign in Egypt, drew up a codicil in his will leaving
him the not inconsiderable sum of £1500. The following year this
gentleman died. Roger could not come into the money until he was
21 so that, no doubt, spurred him on to seek a new protector. This
he found in the form of Count James Frances de Gallatin: 'He was a
bachelor, aged thirty-one, and lived with his mother. He too took to
my soldier father in a big way; soon, indeed, he could hardly bear to
let him out of his sight'.[45] So much so that, having bought the young
man out of the Guards, the Count rented a cottage near the Ackerley
family house in Cheshire and there hosted weekends in which he
entertained the young man as well as another pair (one of whom,
Arthur Stockley, was to introduce Roger to the banana business)
with a variety of indulgences: bathing, poker, 'and whatever athletic
games were available to them'.[46] The Count was clearly infatuated
beyond restraint: a bit later, Roger's career in the wine trade proving
all too modest, he set him up to breed horses in a stables near his
own cottage at Old Windsor. And so, with the complaisance of his
mother, it would seem, the Count and Roger jogged along together
in their 'own quiet way'[47] as coupled as one might imagine until

Miss Louise Burckhardt, a wealthy relation of the Count's family, came from Paris to stay with the de Gallatins. Instead she found Roger; soon enough they were engaged and in September 1889 were married in Paris. Ackerley quotes a letter from Madame de Gallatin to Stockley on the whole business and certainly it makes clear what seems to have been the truth about young Roger:

> I would never have opposed Roger leaving us to try and do better or to *work* but it was the *way* he left us and his *treachery* and all the underhand things he has done – and *more than all* his fearful ingratitude – he has behaved like a coward and a *sneak* – for *I* do not mince matters where justice demands me to speak frankly – He has not moral courage enough to be a friend! And he has sacrificed his best friend and a noble heart for *Money*! This is what I think of him. I forgive him but I can never think well of him again. My son will never be the same.[48]

Yet there is more to this story. Count de Gallatin's 'ghost' entered the son's life. In 1925 while writing *Hindoo Holiday*, Joe Ackerley moved into a flat in Hammersmith.

> Probably from the very beginning, when I first pressed the bell of No. 6 Hammersmith Terrace and Arthur Needham opened the door, I divined that he was homosexual, or as we put it, 'one of us', 'that way', 'so', or 'queer'. One soon got a sense for such recognitions. But with my fear of interruptions and distractions I did not wish to know more, certainly not to claim kinship with him . . . . Recognizing me one evening when he was on duty in King Street as the author of *The Prisoners of War*, which had lately been produced and he had seen, [a policeman] became a friend of mine and got me going socially in Hammersmith much faster than I could ever have got on by myself. Soon No. 6 was being visited by him and other policemen, his selected friends, as well as by sundry pet tradesboys and costermongers whom he had discovered in the course of his day or night duties. Old Arthur, whose lair was on the ground floor, would often answer the bell (I had no bell of my own) and, after the first shock of finding uniformed policemen on his doorstep, much enjoyed the excitement and vicarious pleasure of admitting these youthful, friendly callers.[49]

Within this outré environment, the days passed in literary endeavour clear of old Arthur. But a connection was there which couldn't
be overlooked: on the walls of the staircase hung a particularly large
amateurish

> oil-painting of a pompous old gentleman dressed in ceremonial
> attire and seated on a kind of throne. He had bulging blue eyes
> and a large moustache that extended beyond the sides of his face
> and, waxed at the points, turned upwards like the Kaiser's. A
> pale aristocratic hand, issuing from the folds of his vice-regal
> robes, rested on the arm of his throne. How was I to know that
> this old gentleman was the Count James Francis de Gallatin, my
> father's boyhood friend?[50]

The very same: he had lived round the corner. Not only that, the
Count was most certainly 'that way'; a frequenter of the Napoleon
public house, a well-known place for older men interested in
younger members of the Brigade of Guards. This information
Ackerley first took in while his father was still alive; to that extent
it passed unregistered as it were: after all old Roger was

> simply my old familiar dad, with his large top-heavy figure, his
> Elder Statesman look, his Edward VII hat, umbrella, and eternal
> cigar, his paunch, his moustache, his swivel eye, his jumps and
> his unsteady gait, his dull commuting, respectable life, his
> important business, his dreary office pals, and their eternal
> yarning about chaps putting their hands up girls' frocks (never
> into boys' flies) – it was difficult enough, as I have said, to think
> of him in any amorous situation at all; to imagine him in the arms
> of another man was not possible.[51]

It was only after his death in 1929 that, clearly enmeshed within
the life of the father, Joe began to think it through from the obvious
other angle. For he too was a frequenter of the Napoleon, he too was
attracted by the company of young guardsmen.

> In the thirties I found myself concentrating my attention more
> and more upon a particular society of young men in the metropo-
> lis which I had tapped before and which, it seemed to me, might

yield, without further loss of time, what I required. His Majesy's Brigade of Guards had a long history in homosexual prostitution. Perpetually short of cash, beer, and leisure occupations, they were easily to be found of an evening in their red tunics standing about in the various pubs they frequented, over the only half-pint they could afford or some 'quids-in' mate had stood them, in Knightsbridge, Victoria, the Edgware Road and elsewhere, or hanging about Hyde Park and the Marble Arch, with nothing to do and nothing to spend, whistling therefore in vain to the passing 'prossies', whom they contemptuously called 'bags' (something into which something is put), and alert to the possibility that some kind gentleman might appear and stand them a few pints, in return for which and the subsequent traditional tip – a pound was the recognized tariff for the Foot Guards then, the Horse Guards cost rather more – they were perfectly agreeable to, indeed often eager for, a 'bit of fun'. In their availability and for other reasons they suited my book; though generally larger than I liked, they were young, they were normal, they were working-class, they were drilled to obedience; though not innocent for long, the new recruit might be found before someone else got at him; if grubby they could be bathed, and if civility and consideration, with which they did not always meet in their liaisons, were extended to them, one might gain their affection.

Evening after evening, for many years, when I was free I prowled Marble Arch, the Monkey Walk and Hyde Park Corner, or hastened from pub to pub as one unrewarding scene replaced another. Seaport towns also (sailors too were jolly and short of cash) were often combed at weekends. The taint of prostitution in these proceedings nevertheless displeased me and must, I thought, be disagreeable to the boys themselves, accept it though they did. I therefore developed mutually face-saving techniques to avoid it, such as standing drinks and giving cash at once and, without any suggestive conversation, leaving the boy free to return home with me if he wished, out of sexual desire or gratitude, for he was pretty sure to know what I was after. This, I suppose, was akin to my father's technique of bribery in advance for special restaurant service, for of course I too hoped for responsiveness to generosity and was annoyed if I did not get it. A similar but more self-restrained and hazardous form of procedure was to treat the soldier, if he was particularly

attractive, to a pleasant evening's entertainment – cinema, sup-
per – give him a present at the end of it when he had to return
to barracks, and leave it to him to ask, 'When can I see you again?'
Thus, by implying that it was more his society than his body that
interested me, did I hope to distinguish myself from the other
'twanks' (as guardsmen called people like myself) and gain his
respect. If he did not turn up to his future appointment I was
upset and would loiter about his barracks for days. These meth-
ods had another advantage: they disarmed, or could be hoped
to disarm, any tendency the guardsman might have to robbery
or violence. Such incidents were not frequent but they occurred,
sometimes brutal (the homosexual who was found murdered, his
penis severed and stuck into his own mouth), sometimes jolly
(the Hammersmith queen, who, robbed by a guardsman of his
fur coat, flew out in a rage and found a policeman, who quickly
recovered the conspicuous garment and went to bed with the
grateful owner himself).[52]

So imagine the time-warp and an old Joe rogering a young Roger:
figuring this most perplexing pattern, as Ackerley himself realized,
becomes an exercise in self-generating irony. Miss Burckhardt
died in 1892 and later that year – on the packet to France – the
polished young widower with £2000, annually, picked up Joe's
mother and within three years had her carrying the unwanted
unfortunate Peter. He got round to marrying her the year after
the War ended – that is, a year after the child Peter's death. The
Count de Gallatin in old age might be shrugged aside: '"A funny
chap, a decent sort of fellow, most unfortunately jealous"'[53] but of
Muriel and her daughters Helen, Diana and 'Stella' and their lives
old Roger said nothing. The other family, his other family, was a
secret from his wife and son which he took to the grave. Only after
the event did Joe learn the truth:

> Now for the 'secret orchard' part of my story. For many years I
> had a mistress and she presented me with twin girls ten years
> ago and another girl eight years ago. The children are alive and
> are very sweet things and very dear to me. They know me only
> as Uncle Bodger, but I want them to have the proceeds of my
> Life Insurance of £2,000 (fully paid up and now worth £2,500) in
> the Caledonian Insurance Coy; the policy being with my private
> papers in the safe here. I would also like £500 paid to their

mother. She still keeps her maiden name and doesn't live with the children. You will now begin to realize why I didn't keep a car!! I am not going to make any excuses, old man. I have done my duty towards everybody as far as my nature would allow and I hope people generally will be kind to my memory. All my men pals know of my second family and of their mother, so you won't find it difficult to get on their track.

Your old Dad.[54]

And this is what the son felt:

The discovery of my father's duplicity gave me, I suppose, something of a jolt, not severe to a mind as self-centred as mine, a jolt which gradually intrigued and then engaged my thought more and more as the years passed. It was the kind of shock that people must receive when some old friend, who has just spent with them an apparently normal evening, goes home and puts his head in the gas-oven. The shock, after the shock of death, is the shock to complacency, to self-confidence: the old friend was a stranger after all, and where lay the fault in communication? My relationship with my father was in ruins; I had known nothing about him at all. The 'grown man with every sign of a great intelligence' who, in his posthumous letter, had stood before him on the morning of 21 October 1920 [the date of its composition], the year after his belated secret marriage to my mother, had had, it seemed, insufficient intelligence, then and thereafter, to take him in, to make him out, and to the 'kindly nature towards human frailties' that he had believed me to possess, his own frailties were not entrusted. All his 'men pals', who deserted him at the end like the proverbial rats on the sinking ship, had been let into his 'secret orchard'. I was to join this group 'only in case of my death'.

Why? The question vaguely teased and discomfited my thought, whenever it turned to him, as time went on, and became at last the *raison d'être* of this examining and self-examining book; not the only *raison d'être*, it must be admitted, for, being a writer, I perceived that I had a good story to tell, a story which, as it ramified, grew better and better.[55]

What does one ever know? Or want to know? That is Hamlet's problem with Gertrude. And yet the question isn't as straightforward as Ackerley would perhaps have it. For surely here is one of the truths in the book, a truth about our deceptions (deceptions not just on the social level of norms and conventions) and a truth about the manner and matter of secrets – that old Roger in the end was another kind of prisoner: the secret orchard being both escape and a confinement never to be acknowledged. And wasn't there also the matter of the injuries done to others? Or was there? To what extent was Joe Ackerley's life – above all his creative life – transformed by the father's duplicity? His own life was, of course, necessarily double. But when one ponders the relation of father to son it is almost as if in the end the father had *wanted* something to be made out of it all. Joe Ackerley's literary executor, Francis King, observes that perhaps because of his 'single-minded obsession with the truth that he could never – as he himself often admitted – invent.'[56] And in *Hindoo Holiday* there is the following exchange:

> 'And why do you tell me these secret things?' I asked him mischievously. 'I thought you did not care to hear secret things repeated?'
> 'But you are my friend,' he said, looking at me in surprise; 'so I must say you everything, everything. Is that not good?'
> 'That is very good,' I replied quickly, for I wanted to hear everything, everything.[57]

Of course the failure to invent may itself be an invention. All of his work is crafted: the very structure of *My Father and Myself* is an intricate pattern of revelations (Auden is clearly irritated enough by the ravelling, to present the chronologies of son and father side by side on the page in his review of the work – to no effect) and Ackerley himself writes in the 'Foreword' of 'ploughing to and fro over my father's life and my own, turning up a little more sub-soil each time as the plough turned'. Indeed, for there are not just the revelations about the father to re-organize but also those which the son would or would not reveal about *himself* to the father. Certainly at odds with the apparently indolent unproductive creative writer of the time in the Richmond house was the actual young reporter: the son kept notebooks of life with father (and later copious diaries of life with Tulip, and his sister Nancy) as if, one supposes, he was all along ready just in case a story (he refers again and again to the fact of the 'story' he has to write of his father's secrets) were to present itself. The notebook observations operate in retrospect – in Ackerley's retrospect – ironically since whatever is understood at any one time with certainty reveals, in some distant moment, quite its opposite. The comic is forever disguising its tragic twin, so:

> *Myself* (to my father who has come down to breakfast a little late): How are you?
> *My father*: Rotten night.
> *Myself*: Your jumps again?
> *My father*: Yes. All night.
> *Myself*: Where?
> *My father* (indicating the region of the heart): Here. But it's nothing much. Only a nerve. Damned annoying though. (He moves unsteadily over to the barometer to study the day's weather.) Did I tell you that story Bilson told me the other day? There was a fellow walking down the street when he saw a pretty girl - Ah! damn you! Why can't you let up? – in a very short dress bending down to adjust her garter. So as he passed he put his hand up under her skirt between her legs. She was furious at this. 'How dare you!' she said, but he passed on with a – Crikey! – a smile. So she called a policeman. 'Constable!' she said. 'Arrest that man! He's insulted me!' 'What's he done?' asked the policeman. She told him. 'Well,' said the policeman, 'I'm afraid the evidence isn't sufficient. You'll – Oh, drat the thing! – you'll have to come back with me to the station so that I can photograph the finger-prints.' Te-he-he. . . .[58]

For the jumps – it turns out – were the preliminary symptoms of tertiary syphilis, the disease which eventually killed the old philanderer. All odds evened.

And yet, again, we want to know how much – along with Joe here – he, old Roger, knew of Joe's secrets. There is the following, typical in its bizarre insistence that all should be known and yet, even as the suggestion is toyed with, its secret alternative – the defensive mask of Joe's evidently beautiful face – is being described.

> Could he have conceived that, so far as I was concerned and in spite of my 'kindly nature towards human frailties', I would have been morally shocked, embarrassed, even censorious? Did he

think I would reproach him? Indeed I *would* have reproached
him – for failing, in the chance he had, to provide me with
some more brothers instead of all those extra sisters. What a
thrilling present that would have seemed to me then, some
brand-new teen-age brothers! They might even have yielded the
Ideal Friend! How *could* he have viewed me, this ex-guardsman
with his 'secret orchards' and way of life as shady as my own?
My half-sisters believed that he and their mother, who also
met my sailor in Southsea, realized that I was 'queer', but they
could not have known that I was a practising homosexual, and
I wonder whether, with my 'highbrow' intellectuality, my lack
of interest in girls, my obvious preference for the company
of working-class 'lads', I could so have fogged him, so have
presented myself to him, that he supposed me to be a sort of
social worker, an idealist, a selfless, high-minded fellow remote
from and superior to himself. I have reason to believe that I
often wear a frown. Our public faces can be known to us only
by hearsay and I have been given several clues to my own. A
preoccupied anxious look seems to be my most settled guise,
tinged by sadness. A charming smile: 'sunshine through tears',
someone once described it to me. My fine blue eyes can emit
a piercing stare, I am told, though what on earth they pierce
I have no notion, they certainly did not manage to pierce my
father.[59]

But equally there were moments when father and son might have
made it all plain each to the other. The exchanges are, in their own
ways, enigmatic draws; stand-offs between generations. The old
man, after all, knew what he wasn't talking about:

A constant visitor was a retired air-commodore, L. E. O.
Charlton, with a charming young male companion, not quite
of the same class, to whom he sometimes referred as his secretary,
though one might have wondered why he should need one; there
were also a young actor, who rendered my father momentarily
speechless at dinner one evening by asking him, 'Which do you
think is my best profile, Mr Ackerley' – turning his head from
side to side – 'this, or this?'; a brilliant talkative Irishman, of
encyclopaedic knowledge, with a thin, carefully curled, cylin-
drical fringe of a moustache and black paint round the lower

lids of his eyes, which looked like mascara but was said to be an ointment for conjunctivitis, who arrived in a leather jacket with a leopard-skin collar and pointed purple suede shoes, and lectured my astonished father on the problem of the uneconomic banana skin; and an intellectual policeman. 'Interesting chap,' said my father afterwards, adding, 'It's the first time I've ever entertained a policeman at my table.'[60]

Or more dramatically there was the Turin incident. Loitering about Italy with a lover picked up on the return from India, Ackerley, guilty and nervous of paternal disapproval, passed a message on through a mutual friend that he was directly returning to England but by way of a stopover in Weybridge – you see – with the above mutual friend. And then, of course, he loitered and loafed about Turin with the lover (of which *séjour* he reports to remember nothing) while his father – alas; life is all timing – had a heart-attack at table:

> Dr Wadd, summoned by my mother – the occasion when her prompt action saved my father's life – dashed in with a hypodermic syringe of digitalis and jabbed it so hastily, though successfully, into the back of one of his hands that it raised a large lump which he kept to the end of his days. My mother wired to me in Weybridge: my friend there was not on the phone. Realizing that the game was up, he came over to Richmond and told her the truth. It was decided to keep it from my father and a wire was sent to me in Turin. I never got it, for I was already on my way home; I had suddenly recollected that my birthday was about to fall and foresaw muddlement between Richmond and Weybridge. I did not know of my father's illness, therefore, until I reached the house.
>
> Unfortunately there was something else I did not know; serious flooding had occurred in the Thames valley. I found my father recovering but still bed-ridden; he asked me at once whether the floods had held me up. I looked perfectly blank. Somehow we got round this for the moment, but I saw I had given myself away. I was upset about him, grieved to see him ill, remorseful for having lied to him. A day or two later, when he was better able to talk, I went to him and said, 'I've got something to tell you, Dad. I lied to you about Weybridge. I didn't go there at all.' He said, 'I know, old boy. I knew you were lying directly

I asked you about the floods.' I said, 'I went to Turin.' 'Turin, eh?' he said. 'That's rather farther,' and then, 'I'm very sorry to have mucked up your plans.' This was sickening. I said, 'I'm very sorry to have lied to you. I wouldn't have done so if you hadn't once said something about me and my waiter friends. But I don't really mind telling you. I went to meet a sailor friend. . . .' But he interrupted me with 'It's all right, old boy. I prefer not to know. So long as you enjoyed yourself, that's the main thing.' Thus did he close the door in my face. At that moment, perhaps through some guilty need to confess, I would, for better or for worse, have told him anything in the world.[61]

The final failure of truth, the retreat into crucial silence, is Ackerley's own. Lifting his eyes up from the manuscript of *Hindoo Holiday* (and surely that suggests something more unstated about the relationship) Roger asked, '"Was the Maharajah a bugger?"' 'I wish I had said yes' Ackerley notes.[62] For, of course, he was, but it was the word to which, at that stage of his own sexual career, the son objected. 'I said no and closed the door on him'.

'[H]e asked no questions, invited no confidence – and offered none; if I had my secret life, he had his'.[63] But there is still something perverse about it. After his father died, Joe burned the desk – the only repository it would seem of all his father's personal documents. And again, for all his own assertion of truthfulness there was the whole self-protective need to lie. 'And I dislike lying, though I have got used to it now in the course of years.'[64]

Secret lives – father and son: more different they could not be. One of sedate bourgeois heterosexuality, twice over, with no doubt as many 'plump little partridges' as necessary on the side; the other a solitary, promiscuously cruising pubs and streets. One, having negotiated his own amoral pacts with existence, nonetheless remained caught within webs of deceit – Ackerley's mother never, to his knowledge, knew of the secret orchard. The other desperately seeking what, in the end, all of Ackerley's writing confronts, and confronts in a most morally perplexing and distressing way, the satisfactions, if such they be, of love; the release from the selfishness of ego through the companionship of another, any other living feeling creature; escape.

Yet in spite of such adventures, if anyone had asked me what I was doing I doubt if I should have replied that I was diverting myself. I think I should have said that I was looking for the Ideal Friend. If I had not said that in the beginning I would certainly have said it later. Though two or three hundred young men were to pass through my hands in the course of years, I did not consider myself promiscuous but monogamous, it was all in a run of bad luck, and I became ever more serious over this as time went on. Perhaps as a reaction to my school, Army, and Cambridge difficulties, the anxiety, nervousness, guilt that had dogged me all along the line (though I did not think of it then as guilt, if indeed it was), I was developing theories of life to suit myself: sex was delightful and of prime importance, the distance between the mouth and the crotch must be bridged at once, clothes must come off as soon as possible, no courtship, no nonsense, no beating, so to speak, about the bush, the quickest, perhaps the only, way to get to know anyone thoroughly was to lie naked in bed with him, both were at once disarmed of all disguise and pretence, all cards were on the table and one could tell whether he was the Ideal Friend. What I meant by the Ideal Friend I doubt if I ever formulated, but now, looking back over the years, I think I can put him together in a partly negative way by listing some of his many disqualifications. He should not be effeminate, indeed preferably normal; I did not exclude education but did not want it, I could supply all that myself and in the loved one it had always seemed to get in the way; he should admit me but no one else; he should be physically attractive to me and younger than myself – the younger the better, as closer to innocence; finally he should be on the small side, lusty, circumcised, physically healthy and clean: no phimosis, halitosis, bromidrosis. It may be thought that I had set myself a task so difficult of accomplishment as almost to put success purposely beyond my reach; it may be thought too that the reason why this search was taking me out of my own class into the working class, yet still towards that innocence which in *my* class I had been unable to touch, was that guilt in sex obliged me to work it off on my social inferiors. This occurred to me only as a latter-day question and the answer may be true, I cannot tell; if asked then I would probably have said that working-class boys were more unreserved and understanding, and that friendship with them opened up interesting areas of life, hitherto unknown.[65]

But when a friend once asked him whether he ever 'lost himself' in sex, the answer had to be no. For he never did find the 'permanent' Ideal Friend: not in human form at least.

IX

And now we come to the hard part.

We have to start again with the fact that Ackerley's relation to life was to an extent decidedly voyeuristic: this can be politely redefined as a taste for domestic anthropology:

> In the mid thirties I began to keep a day-to-day diary. I had developed another of my theories – self-defensive it now looks – that there was not the slightest need to seek material for travel books, as writers usually did, by going off to foreign parts, climbing mountains, living with primitive tribes, pioneering down untrodden paths if any were left; everyone's life, said I, even the veriest bank clerk's in Manchester or Little Pidlington, was crammed with the most exciting interest and adventure if only he would observe and describe it. Let anyone keep a candid, detailed diary for a year, noting down *everything* that happened to him day by day, in his life, in his mind, and a book would emerge far more fascinating, however clumsily written, than if he had been anthropologizing among the Pygmies or sliding about on Arctic ice. My own diary lasted some six months, hastily scrawled because my nocturnal ramblings, all described, took up so much of my time. Then I got bored and discontinued it.[66]

This then was a second set of diaries written presumably to satisfy a deep need. Indeed later, after the second war, he was to keep a further journal detailing his relationship with his sister: a journal[67] which repeats the themes of his nature; from the recurrent sense of inadequacy and hence guilt – Nancy attempted suicide – to the compensatory release through love. And it seems that the evidently compulsive act of writing (writing primarily for whom indeed: oneself?) with its prima facie insistence on truth may in fact become an act of love, if only by revealing the possibility that there might be – after it all – some kind of ennobling esteem of self. The guilt is the motive force; the confession the release; the tacit relationship with the reader the absolution. The conclusion to the paragraph quoted above is this:

Fifteen years later I came upon it again, read it through and instantly destroyed it, as though it were an evil thing. The evil was in the misery. It contained no single gleam of pleasure or happiness, no philosophy, not even a joke; it was a story of unrelieved gloom and despondency, of deadly monotony, of frustration, loneliness, self-pity, of boring 'finds', of wonderful chances muffed through fear, of the latchkey turned night after night into the cold, dark, empty flat, of railings against fate for the emptiness and wretchedness of my life. It also contained, the saddest thing of all, my critical comments upon my first meeting with that Welsh boy, now dead, his dullness and smelly feet.[68]

'He once astonished me' relates Francis King 'by prefacing one of his remarks with "To an outcast like me. . ." I had never thought of anyone of such aristocracy of demeanour and spirit as possibly being an outcast'.[69] It may be that there is too much self-contempt behind this remark for it not to be more honestly cited as self-pity. Yet, if only for the fact of his homosexuality, we must assent to an objective truth in Ackerley's observation: his desires led him beyond the law. But then again, in his specific case, this can only offer a partial explanation. The realization that his family lived within isolated exclusion – that life is in truth about not opening one's heart, not sharing, not trusting – must have been peculiarly hurtful. Nonetheless, the malaise – in its unredeemed condition – lies deeper within the affections and loyalties of his family, lies, *au fond*, in the dead brother's grave, within the dead brothers of the War. The sense of exile can only be related to a misanthropic understanding of human life which in turn is a response to the religious sense of man's hideously fallen nature. So that there is an idealized belief in the overwhelming need for love and the empirical observation that nowhere can this love be satisfied. In the first instance, then, the experiences of the War – particularly the trauma of Peter Ackerley's death – create a generally inescapable belief in the utter negation of all human potential for creation. In that sense, the intense desire for freedom – for creation – is explicitly the moral truth of Ackerley's work. Following *The Prisoners of War*, the travel diaries which make up *Hindoo Holiday* rework and repeat these themes. The book is prefaced with this 'Explanation':

He wanted someone to love him – His Highness, I mean; that was his real need I think. He alleged other reasons, of course – an

English private secretary, a tutor for his son; for he wasn't really
a bit like the Roman Emperors and had to make excuses.

The journal is conventionally observational in an anthropological
sense: there is a full narrative of life with the Maharajah, of the different castes and sects surrounding him including the European – so
that the book's type is familiar to us in its Forsterean versions: *A
Passage to India* and *The Hill of Devi*. But the heart of its life is in the
strong emotional response to the multitude of taboos structuring
Indian culture. The prohibitions on physical contact, because of
dietetic and sanitary ordinances, clearly distress Ackerley while
there runs throughout the narrative (as Roger observed) a thrill
of homoerotic pleasure, (the Maharajah indeed liked boys) with a
rather Whitmanesque insistence upon the genuinely promiscuous
acceptance of created reality: 'Give me the unhygienic customs of
Europe! Give the loving cup! Give me the kiss!' [70]

When I returned to the encampment in the dusk, Narayan came
down the path to meet me. I thought how graceful he looked in
his white muslin clothes, the sleeves of his loose vest widening
out at the wrist, the long streamers of his turban floating behind
him. The breeze puffed at his *dhoti* as he approached, moulding
the soft stuff to the shape of his thigh; then as he turned a bend
in the path another gentle gust took the garment from behind and
blew it aside, momentarily baring a slim brown leg. I took his
hand and led him into my tent, and he told me that His Highness
had invited him to return to the New *Bakhri*, but that he feared
to do so lest he should be treated with disrespect, and anyway it
did not matter much because he liked being with me.
    'I want to love you very much,' he said.
    'You mean you do love me very much.'
    'I want to.'
    'Then why not?'
    'You will go to England and I shall be sorry. But you will not
be sorry. I am only a boy and I shall be sorry.'
    When he got up to go, he asked me not to accompany
him as usual to the fair-ground where he meets Sharma,
but to let him go back alone this evening; then before I had
time to reply, he suddenly laughed softly and drew me after
him. And in the dark roadway, overshadowed by trees, he put
up his face and kissed me on the cheek. I returned his kiss;
but he at once drew back, crying out:

'Not the mouth! You eat meat! You eat meat!'

'Yes, and I will eat you in a minute,' I said, and kissed him on the lips again, and this time he did not draw away.[71]

X

But then again, in its turn, England, a culture riddled with taboos and castes – with its separations of class, its inhibitions and prohibitions, its hypocrisy and meanness – equally became an inversion of the ideal. Love turned into the miserable scroll of endless pursuit; of 'the latchkey turned night after night into the cold, dark, empty, flat' railing against one's fate, against the emptiness of the unrealized Ideal Friend. Yet even that may seem a simplification of Ackerley's own relationship to his sexual subculture, to the complex and disturbing crossovers of class and desire. The perversion of unrestricted pleasure through the descent into self-contempt at having scenes with men you despise; the condescensions to those who are 'socially inferior', certainly creates conditions for isolation, loneliness, self-confinement; so much so that, in the end, it had to come to an end. He gave up human-kind: love, ardent affection, that emotional state on the other side of friendship, could be found only in the shape of Queenie, also known as Evie or finally Tulip – to whom *My Father and Myself* is dedicated – his Alsatian bitch:

This bitch of mine entered my life in the middle forties and entirely transformed it. I have already described her in two books; it is necessary to say here that I don't believe there was anything special about her, except that she was rather a beauty. In this context it is not she herself but her effect upon me that I find interesting. She offered me what I had never found in my sexual life, constant, single-hearted, incorruptible, uncritical devotion, which it is in the nature of dogs to offer. She placed herself entirely under my control. From the moment she established herself in my heart and home, my obsession with sex fell wholly away from me. The pubs I had spent so much of my time in were never revisited, my single desire was to get back to her, to her waiting love and unstaling welcome. So urgent was my longing every day to rejoin her that I would often take taxis part-way, even the whole way, home to Putney from my London office, rather than endure the dawdling of buses and the rush-hour traffic jams in Park Lane. I sang with joy at the thought of seeing her. I never prowled the London streets again, nor had the slightest inclination to do so. On the contrary, whenever I thought of it, I was positively thankful to be rid of it all, the anxieties, the frustrations, the wastage of time and spirit. It was as though I had never wanted sex at all, and that this extraordinary long journey of mine which had seemed a pursuit of it had really been an attempt to escape from it. I was just under fifty when this animal came into my hands, and the fifteen years she lived with me were the happiest of my life.[72]

And in truth this was to all intents and purposes a kind of marriage. He had found the Ideal Friend – a female one, moreover – in a beast. The question, of course, that poses itself immediately, given the intensity of feeling expressed, is anticipated by Ackerley himself:

> One of my friends, puzzled by the sudden change in my ways, asked me whether I had sexual intercourse with her. It may be counted as something on the profit side of my life that I could not receive such a question intelligently. I said no.[73]

Nonetheless in reading *My Dog Tulip*, the biography of Queenie, it becomes clear that he was intimately concerned with the dog's sexuality, in her reproductive life, her heats. There are passages of fascinating detail on the travails of breeding, littering and, later, frustrating reproduction. As Ackerley quietly notes, the reality of Tulip is found not in the possible salacious discovery of a physically perverse relationship by the reader but in the emotional truths (or are these to be deemed perverse?) figured by his infatuation. For, on one level, it seems perfectly clear: the dog runs free, the dog is the essence of liberation from all the treachery and constraints found in humanity. It has the truth of bestiality, of nature unaccommodated, offering the illusion of real existence, cutting past the imprisonments of taboos and prejudices:

> We are safe. We are free. The bus trundles up Putney High Street and stops alongside No. 2 The Pines. Up Putney Hill it goes, and now we are running by the edge of the Common. We can dismount anywhere here, but there are some points better avoided – rangers' cottages and their dogs – and in time I know

all the safest tracks. Once over the road we are among trees and bracken, lost to the world of dogs and of men. Crossing the open plateau with its golf course, we give a wide berth to the Windmill, where Lord Cardigan fought his duel in 1840, where Lord Baden-Powell wrote part of his *Scouting for Boys* in 1908, and descend into the birch woods on the far slopes.

This is our goal, our haven. Here, where the silver trees rise in their thousands from a rolling sea of bracken, Tulip turns into the wild beast she resembles. Especially at this early hour the beautiful, remote place must reek of its small denizens, and the scent of the recent passage of rabbits and squirrels, or the sound of the nervous beating of their nearby hidden hearts, throws her into a fever of excitement. The bracken is shoulder high, but soon she is leaping over it. Round and round she goes, rhythmically rising and falling, like a little painted horse in a roundabout, her fore-legs flexed for pouncing, her tall ears pricked and focused, for she has located a rabbit in a bush. Useless to go straight in after it, she has learnt that; the rabbit simply dives out the other side and is lost. Her new technique is cleverer and more strenuous. She must be everywhere at once. She must engirdle the crafty, timid creature and confuse it with her swiftness so that it knows not which way to turn. And barking is unwisdom, she has discovered that too, for although it may add to the general terrorizing effect of her tactic, it also hinders her own hearing of the tiny, furtive movement in the midst of the bush. Silently, therefore, or with only a muted whimpering of emotion, she rises and falls, effortlessly falls and rises, like a dolphin out of the green sea among the silver masts, herself the colour of their bark, battling her wits with those of her prey. The rabbit can bear no more and makes its dart; in a flash, with a yelp, she is after it, streaking down the narrow track. Rabbits are agile and clever. This one flies, bounds, doubles, then bounces like a ball and shoots off at right angles. But Tulip is clever too. She knows now where the burrows lie and is not to be hoodwinked. The rabbit has fled downhill to the right; she sheers off to the left, and a tiny scream pierces the quiet morning and my heart. Alas, Tulip has killed![74]

Yes, but then again that isn't the truth of it either: the dog is ours, it 'belongs' to us, it has a name, it is ordered, curbed, trained, rewarded and punished by us. And this Ackerley acknowledges also: there is a passage near the end of the American edition of *My Dog Tulip*, which meditates on the canine condition.

> Whatever breed or no-breed they might be, they seemed too preposterous or indistinct beside the wild beauty of my imperial bitch; but I saw how amiable and well-mannered they mostly were, in a way how sad, above all how nervous with their air of surreptitious guilt, and meeting the mild, worried brown eyes that often studied me and my friendly hand with doubt, I realized clearly, perhaps for the first time, what strained and anxious lives dogs must lead, so emotionally involved in the world of men, whose affections they strive endlessly to secure, whose authority they are expected unquestioningly to obey, and whose mind they never can do more than imperfectly reach and comprehend. Stupidly loved, stupidly hated, acquired without thought, reared and ruled without understanding, passed on or 'put to sleep' without care, did they, I wondered, these descendants of the creatures who, thousands of years ago in the primeval forests, laid siege to the heart of man, took him under their protection, tried to tame him, and failed – did they suffer from headaches?[75]

And further, here is the entry from *My Sister and Myself* for 11 October, 1950:

> Be kind to dogs, dear reader; they deserve your sympathy and even gratitude. For they are the universal consoler. The love which was once lavished upon you or which you once so ardently sought and then found insufferable and escaped from, it is all now lavished on them. They have taken your place, and enable you to live in carefree independence and freedom elsewhere. But for them there is no escape. To extricate yourself from the possessive, jealous and interfering clutches of wife, mummy, sister or mistress, a number of course were open to you – the army, the colonies, murder, the divorce court, or simply the train and desertion. But poor doggie, the universal consoler *malgré lui*, has no such means. He mops up for you, in the slobber on his coat, the eternal tears of the world, tears of frustrated love, of grief, of rage, which you have caused to flow. That love from which you fled with a shudder, he is the substitute victim of it now. Anything you revolted against – loss of freedom, nagging,

jealousy, emotional scenes and so on – the whole bag of tricks is your legacy to him. Do not hate or despise him: he is your saviour; he earns your pity and gratitude.

So when you see a lady dragging a little dog along on a string, think to yourself, 'There, but for the grace of God, go I.'[76]

So are we to believe this description – our dogs are our prisoners, our pathetic victims? Surely this is a perverse reading of a common fact of life: the human and natural world in some kind of symbiotic agreement to their mutual advantage? Perhaps: but this entry needs to be set against a later observation:

Upon the concrete verandah the bars of my cage are cast, cast by the sun as it sinks below the balustrades. How pretty the pattern they make, the bars of my cage. They lie beside me, bars of shadow, bars of brightness, on the concrete ground, they lie upon my body as I sit in my deck chair and upon the body of my dog beside me. We are within our cage together, the cage we have chosen, as happy as it is possible to be with death drawing closer.[77]

Is that perverse? Or this?

Yet looking at her sometimes I used to think that the Ideal Friend, whom I no longer wanted, perhaps never had wanted, should have been an animal-man, the mind of my bitch, for instance, in the body of my sailor, the perfect human male body always at one's service through the devotion of a faithful and uncritical beast.[78]

Perverse indeed. Surely this is a bizarre redefinition of Gulliverian misanthropy: a virulent view of life, for Gulliver – being so driven by his revulsion at human 'bestiality' – fell to despair and attempted suicide. Was Ackerley too in despair? For *Gulliver's Travels* – 'a savage book' – was 'very much my own view of the world'.[79] He married his dog. In the biography of Queenie we read an extended love letter: his descriptions of her emotional and physical life have a gaiety and wit of the infatuated. The illusion of freedom (even when the dog's desires are repressed, the man knows and cares, takes moral decisions about her life, broods on her well-being) is sustained against all contradiction. In the book's conclusion, there is an extended melancholic contemplation upon suicides on Putney Common, true:

> . . . day after day I uncover it and root it up, this disease in the heart of life. I dispose it where it can do least harm; I bury it at the foot of the trees, I cast it into the midst of the densest thorn or furze. But not into this holly thicket, for last year a man entered it to die. So deep did he burrow into his green unwelcoming shroud that it was many days before his body was found, his empty phial beside him. Not at the foot of this oak, with its curtsying stem and long proffered arm . . . Again the choice was made. Who made it? Carrying his rope with him from Kingston at night, he moved up through the dark woods, clambered here and dropped off into space. It gave the ranger who found him 'quite a turn' to see him standing there, his feet off the ground, so steady and so still. Who? Why? The failed, the frustrated lives pass on, leaving no trace. The place must be full of ghosts . . . And young Holland, where did he die? Where is the swamp into which he drove his face? Lost, lost, the inconsiderable, anguished deed in the blind hurry of time. The perfect boy face downwards in a swamp . . . The doctor who performed the autopsy remarked that the muscles and limbs were absolutely perfect, he had never seen a better developed boy in his life, nor, when he split open the skull, such deep grey matter.[80]

But this is balanced by the necessary illusion of happiness, of purpose even in the midst of purposelessness –

> The cold night mists are still dissolving from the naked grove. The ground is brittle with frost. Out of their ragged green trousers the huge legs of the giant birch sprawl above my head. I pause for a moment upon his crutch and gaze fearfully upward. It looks no worse, the black mark and the thin trickle of blood, too high to reach, too high for my eyes at first to be sure, until I perceived the repulsive white fungi, like brackets, sprouting about it. He is sick, the great tree, he is doomed. It is a secret between us, but not for long will he escape the woodman's notice. They will cut off his legs, I think, as I pass between them prodding for glass. They will throw him down, the lord of the woods, they will throw him down, I say to myself as I linger at the edge of the grove looking back. There is a sudden scurry

of noise, and Tulip flies across the ride on which I stand, her nose to the ground. Out of the tattered undergrowth on one side, into the tattered undergrowth on the other, she rushes; she has come, she has gone, silence claps down again, it is as though she never had been. Excepting that, caught upon the cinders of the ride in front of me curls and wavers in the frozen air the warm white fume of her breath. I watch it as it clings, writhes, wavers, slowly dissolves. She has been, she has gone, nothing now remains. Soon it will be over. Soon it will be too late . . .⁸¹

– which runs counter to any Swiftian madness; for here is love, albeit a melancholy love, of existence. Here is meaning. And if Ackerley had thus let matters rest one could be happy to believe that at least the illusion survives: why should we demand that he like or be like us? But then there is the admission in *My Father and Myself* of this understanding's imaginative anticipation:

At the time when I read this diary I was happy at last. It is, for me, the interesting part of this personal history that peace and contentment reached me in the shape of an animal, an Alsatian bitch. Is it, I wonder, of any value as a clue to my psychology to recall that in my play *The Prisoners of War* the hero, Captain Conrad (myself of course), unable to build on human relations, takes to a plant? He tells some story of another imprisoned officer who fell in love with a pet rabbit and read short stories to it out of a magazine. 'Plants or rabbits,' he says, 'it's the same thing.'⁸²

And there are equally the observations of those who knew Ackerley and Queenie, suggesting, alas, a quite different story and one which hardly bears thinking about:

All three of Joe's women – Aunt Bunny, Nancy, Queenie – were jealous of each other; but Bunny, admirable old woman that she was, with her jaunty, slightly raffish air but her unwavering dignity and decency, differed from the other two in rarely expressing her jealousy. As the diaries will show, Joe was far fonder of the bitch than of the two humans. All Joe's friends, even those who were dog-lovers like myself, hated Queenie. 'Beastly animal,' Forster once muttered to me, when Joe had left us alone together in his room and the dog, squatting on its haunches on his bed, its ears laid back, had begun to set up a continuous low growl. 'Joe has ruined her – no discipline', was the verdict of John

Morris, a believer in discipline, both for himself and for others. Yet Joe would freely give to this hysterical, capricious animal all the love that he grudged his hysterical, capricious sister. The dog would always follow him into his room; but the sister, having knocked, . . . would often be told, 'Sorry, old dear, we're busy', when all that was keeping Joe busy with some friend like myself was a bottle of wine and gossip.[83]

But what is the important judgement here? That Joe was unkind to his sister or that Joe it was that died: the beast had tamed the man? If so what then? Certainly something deeper and more disturbing, profoundly disturbing, is enacted in the dog's final literary appearance.

We Think the World of You is Ackerley's novel: Evie is at the centre of the emotional struggles it relates. In reality Queenie, Evie is the fictional recreation of the biographical Tulip. What are we to make of the nominal transformations? *My Father and Myself*, Ackerley's last work, is dedicated to the earliest account of Queenie – Tulip. Is the 'fictional' Evie an attempt to rescue the dog from the opprobrium it earned in its real existence: Forster's 'Beastly animal'? Or does Ackerley want to suggest a mythologized victim of forces beyond her control? For certainly the novel is about unmoved authority, punishment and retribution; its overwhelming perception is of a fallen world, an entire culture in chains: the thematic tensions radiate from the realization that all of the characters are prisoners – prisoners of their own characters, prisoners of their needs and desires and demands of each other. Johnny, the dog's owner, has had to leave her, as well as his recently born son, with his parents in order to relieve his pregnant wife's burden of bringing up the remaining child while he completes his sentence of a year's imprisonment in Wormwood Scrubs: done for housebreaking. The *donnée* of the piece, then, is the imprisoned Johnny – pulling at him are parents, a wife, children and one character more: Frank the novel's narrator (and clearly Ackerley) who engages in holding the family's attention through his acts of patronage. It is soon quite clear that Frank had been Johnny's elderly lover (indeed one of Ackerley's own lovers had been sent to prison for housebreaking) and that his engagement with the family is, in truth, not at all in good faith. Frank is still infatuated with Johnny and, using his economic advantages, donates a sum towards the upkeep of the children: thus the sexual and economic counterthrusts (Johnny imprisons Frank sexually and Frank Johnny economically) allow Ackerley to cross from the vague unarticulated world of his own middle class to the underclass of post-war Britain. It is while visiting Johnny's parents that Frank sees Evie: the dog is also a prisoner, trapped in the yard when not stuffed in the scullery, and it is Frank's indignation which causes the plot to unfold. Quite simply it becomes his struggle to win the dog away from Johnny's parents and finally away from Johnny. And, of course, given his financial power he succeeds.

The novel thus unites all of Ackerley's obsessions; for within the struggle to free Evie is the development of Frank's love for the dog. He manages to borrow her for a weekend: the narrative then recounts how he falls in love:

> I would have to go to her; she would not come to me. All the fawning sentiment that had characterised her puppy days had gone. Her love was now aloof. I would call her but she would not come. Motionless as a carven image she would sit, her head drawn back, her glowing eyes fixed tenderly and steadfastly upon me, and I would put my book away and go to her, moved by her love and her beauty. Shoot her indeed!
>
> At night she slept as she pleased, in an arm-chair in my bedroom or on my bed. If she began on the chair she usually ended up on the bed. It was a double bed, and sometimes she would curl up at my feet, but mostly against the pillow, laying down her head beside my own. She was quite odourless; the faint sweet smell, perhaps, of fur or feather. And when the room was darkened she fell asleep at once. In the morning she would wake me by dabbing a paw on my face; sometimes I would be roused to find her lying with all her length upon me, her forearms on my shoulders, looking gaily down into my eyes. Another day had begun. . . .[84]

The need for the dog becomes an obsession: Frank is reduced to pathetic attempts at manipulating Johnny's wife and parents as he tries to get at him, inside prison, to sell the dog. Here he struggles for civility in the face of his most powerful opponent, Megan, Johnny's wife:

> 'Did you see Evie?'
> 'Yes, I saw her.'

My voice broke a little as I asked:
'How was she?'
'She was all right.'
'And nothing was said about her or me at all?'
'No.'
I gave it up.
'Look here,' I said. 'When are you going to see Johnny again?'
'It will be about a fortnight before the next visit comes.'
'Can't you ask for an earlier one on compassionate grounds? I
want to go with you.'
'I've just had one. They wouldn't give me another so soon.'
I stared at her.
'Do you mean you've been *again* since I last saw you?'
'Yes, I went yesterday.'
'I see.' Beyond her shoulder, through a gap in the rep curtains,
the two children were visible crouched together like witches
over their pebbles on the sunlit doorstep. I brought my terrified
gaze back to her with an effort. 'Well, I must really ask to go
with you on the next official visit. It's essential for me to see
Johnny now.'
'They said they was coming next time.'
'The beasts!'
Megan studied me silently. Then she said:
'What does it all matter? It's only a dog.'
For a moment I gazed at her speechlessly.
'Even a dog has a right to its life.'
'There are more important things to think about.'[85]

It is a world of crashing appetites and selfish, desperate desires.
Johnny's parents want to keep their grandchild. Frank, overcome
by a ruling passion, wants to buy the dog. But Johnny has paid for
her with his time – done the houses to raise money for the deposit
on the dog in the first place. With his release the struggle finally
resolves itself through Evie's choice between the two men. Frank
wins her loyalty – as he always would. But with what is he left?
That is the novel's bleak question. Living with Frank, Evie becomes
truly his possession with a 'different way of life' and Johnny, in the
resentment over selling her to him, bows to the obvious demands
of his own heterosexual married life and drifts coldly away. Frank
wins, yes, but what? A beast that dominates his life utterly and
beyond all reason: now without Johnny, the only human contact

left is a cousin who moves in to help run the flat. The dog drives her off, drives her away because the human wanted it.

> . . . I did not want to lose my dog. When I thought of losing her I trembled with the kind of internal cold that seems the presage of death. I loved her; I wished her forever happy; but I could not bear to lose her. I could not bear to share her. She was my true love and I wanted her all to myself.[86]

He becomes a prisoner in his own house: isolated in another kind of war, hideously trapped within a world he has created for himself, a creature of his own desires, a man without any human love. Is this not madness? The darkness of one's own mind?

> Since then she has set herself to keep everyone else out of it. None of the succession of visiting helps I engaged to supply my cousin's place stayed longer than a few days; even the sparrows and pigeons that try to perch on my verandah are instantly put to flight; no fly enters and survives; she would know if I stroked another animal on my way home for she smells me all over directly I return and I should suffer from remorse if I hurt her feelings; she cannot actually read my correspondence, but she seizes it all as it falls through the letter-box and tears it to shreds. Advancing age has only intensified her jealousy. I have lost all my old friends, they fear her and look at me with pity or contempt. We live entirely alone. Unless with her I can never go away. I can scarcely call my soul my own. Not that I am complaining, oh no; yet sometimes as we sit and my mind wanders back to the past, to my youthful ambitions and the freedom and independence I used to enjoy, I wonder what in the world has happened to me and how it all came about. . . . But that leads me into deep waters, too deep for fathoming; it leads me into the darkness of my own mind.[87]

But what is it that unsettles the mind? As Stuart Hampshire noted '[t]he only creature that truly responds is the dog, who does indeed call for human help and who is able to accept it'.[88] And the cliché of the title which runs ironically back and forth through the conversations, used as it is by all of the characters except Frank, can truthfully be held as Evie's view of both her lovers – Frank and Johnny. Nonetheless, as Stuart Hampshire concludes, in his review of the novel, it is 'an eccentric and strange episode of the conversion of love. But a very particular case is turned into a general truth by the art of fiction'.[89] That is because – as he further observes – there is the story to tell and there are the truths of the experiencing consciousnesses. For the unsettling nature of Ackerley's work is that, as we can now see, it consistently achieves positions which might well be called eccentric or – more powerfully alien – having pursued a logic and fidelity to truth-telling which implacably forces the reader back towards the central moral questions of any serious hold on life. Isn't Hampshire absolutely right? These words go beyond any limited sense of sincerity and truthfulness as 'self-expression', reaching instead such an organized control over the elements of its experience as to make us ask: is not this a discovery of 'particular modes of consciousness and of feeling that are here for the first time fully distinguished' which is yet true to 'general experience'?[90]

The darkness of mind is coloured indeed by its own experiences. That the end of the novel reveals a shocking new set of conditions for life – out of emptiness for the briefest most illusory moment, into the imprisonment of emotional plenitude – seems to be exactly of that truthfulness which we find in serious expression. For, if it is the truth of our human societies, our kind, that we are lesser creatures than the beasts in exactly those qualities which we falsely assume make us distinct from them (e.g. love), are we not then bound to contemplate the burden which closes *We Think the World of You* as irredeemably tragic? Ah, but that, one might say, is his problem. And certainly of problems Ackerley had quite enough. Yet it seems equally true that the end of his writing is not concerned with self-pity, not in the least. It has a kind of integrity and calm intelligence – a detachment from self – which puts to one a simple question: but – really – aren't we so? Don't we treat life thus? And that truth may well have had its birth within the nightmare of life in the trenches, observing humanity going about its business as usual. For there is one more anecdote of that time which lies hauntingly behind so much of the later writing: it is recalled in *Hindoo Holiday* – a group of ants is at work dismembering a dead fly:

> Looking down on this gruesome scene, I was suddenly back in the dawn of May 3rd, 1917, advancing under fire with my orderly against the German position in the village of Cérisy in

France. It was twilight, and we were following our barrage up the slope of a hill, darting from shell-hole to shell-hole in short spurts as the curtain of fire lifted and moved forward. Resting in one of these shell-holes in this inferno with my orderly, of whom I was both proud and fond, I noticed a strange movement on the crepuscular skyline of the hill, some fifty yards ahead, and regarding it intently for some time, made it out to be the moving arms of a man, presumably a wounded German, who must be lying on his back. I could not see his body, only the arms, which rose high in the air and fell, rose and fell, in the most strange and desolate rhythm, like a man trying to keep warm in slow motion, or the last wing-beats of a dying bird – or the weak wavings of this fly's legs. Then I noticed that my orderly had left me and was rushing up the slope ahead. I was astonished and angry; his strict duty was at my side. I yelled at him, but he paid no heed – if, indeed, in that appalling racket, he ever heard. What on earth could he be doing? It was soon and shockingly evident. Quite careless, apparently, of danger, which, as he approached our barrage, became doubly grave, I saw him, silhouetted against the flashing explosions, reach and stoop over the wounded German, poke the muzzle of his rifle into the man's body and pull the trigger. The rising arms hovered for a moment, then finally fell. Even then I did not entirely twig, until my orderly came leisurely back to rejoin me, a smile of deep satisfaction on his handsome face, and held out to my inspection a German officer's revolver, field-glasses, wrist-watch and cigarette case. He had murdered the wounded man in order to rob him. 'Souvenir!' he said, smiling at me.[91]

Joe Ackerley, on the other hand, died in his sleep. And sister Nancy almost knocked on the door as she entered his room to show Francis King the body.

How life falls somewhat short of our ideals.[92]

Notes

INTRODUCTION: INVENTING TRADITIONS

1. La Rochefoucauld, *Maximes et Autres Oeuvres Morales* (Paris, 1949) CDXXXVI, p. 73.
2. F. R. Leavis, 'Xenia', in *Eugenio Montale: New Poems* (New York, 1976) p. XXVI.
3. Thomas Gray, 'Sonnet: On the Death of Richard West', *The Poems of Gray and Collins* (Oxford, 1937) p. 130.
4. Eugenio Montale, 'I Travestimenti', *It Depends: A Poet's Notebook (Quaderno di quattro anni)* (New York, 1980) pp. 40–1.
5. La Rochefoucauld, *Maximes*, CCCXVI, p. 58.
6. T. S. Eliot, 'The Three Voices of Poetry', *On Poetry and Poets* (London, 1957) p. 89.
7. E. A. Poe, 'The Imp of the Perverse', *Tales of Mystery and Imagination* (London, 1908) p. 366.
8. T. S. Eliot, *The Waste Land, Collected Poems 1909–1962* (London, 1963) p. 79.
9. Philip Larkin, 'Grub Village', *Required Writing: Miscellaneous Pieces 1955–1982* (London, 1983) p. 190.
10. Edward Thomas, 'In Memoriam (Easter, 1915)', *The Oxford Book of Twentieth Century English Verse* (Oxford, Clarendon Press, 1973; reprinted with corrections 1974) p. 130.
11. Edward Thomas, 'As the Team's Head-Brass', *The Oxford Book of Twentieth Century English Verse*, pp. 129–30.
12. Thomas Hardy, 'In Time of "The Breaking of Nations"', *The Complete Poems* (London, 1976) p. 543.
13. Quoted in Michael Millgate, *Thomas Hardy, A Biography* (Oxford, reprinted with corrections, 1987) p. 516.
14. Georg Simmel, 'The Stranger', *On Individuality and Social Forms, Selected Writings* (Chicago, 1971) p. 143.
15. Ibid., p. 145.
16. See Lesley D. Harman, *The Modern Stranger: On Language and Membership* (Berlin, New York, Amsterdam, 1988) pp. 19–21 for a discussion of Robert E. Park's 'Human Migration and the Marginal Man', *American Journal of Sociology*, 33 (8), pp. 881–93.
17. Quoted in Harman, *The Modern Stranger*, p. 19.
18. Georg Simmel, 'The Stranger', *On Individuality and Social Forms*, p. 145.
19. T. S. Eliot, *The Waste Land, Collected Poems 1909–1962*, p. 67.
20. Ibid., p. 63.
21. Ibid., p. 71.
22. T. S. Eliot, 'Gerontion', *Collected Poems 1909–1962*, p. 39.

23. T. S. Eliot, *Ash Wednesday*, *Collected Poems 1909–1962*, p. 95.
24. William Shakespeare, 'Sonnet 19', *Shakespeare's Sonnets* (New Haven and London) 1977, pp. 26–8.
25. T. S. Eliot, *The Letters of T. S. Eliot, Volume I 1898–1922* (London, 1988) p. 199.
26. F. R. Leavis, *The Great Tradition* (Peregrine Books, 1962) p. 33.
27. For example, consider Professor Hugh Kenner's *A Sinking Island: The Modern English Writers* (sic) (London, 1987). Professor Kenner, author of *The Pound Era*, has never even heard of Edward Thomas, Ivor Gurney, or J. R. Ackerley: or so it would appear from his book.
28. Philip Larkin, 'High Windows', *Collected Poems* (London, 1988) p. 165.
29. Philip Larkin, 'Friday Night in the Royal Station Hotel', *Collected Poems* p. 163.
30. Philip Larkin, 'MCMXIV', *Collected Poems*, pp. 127–8.

CHAPTER 1: THE CHILDHOOD OF EDWARD THOMAS

1. Robert Frost, *Selected Letters* (New York, 1964) p. 216.
2. Edward Thomas, *The Childhood of Edward Thomas: a fragment of autobiography* (London, 1983) p. 60.
3. Quoted in Eleanor Farjeon, *Edward Thomas: The Last Four Years* (Oxford, 1958; reissued 1979) pp. 263–4.
4. Edward Thomas, ['P. H. T'], *The Collected Poems of Edward Thomas* (Oxford, Clarendon Press, 1978) p. 273.
5. Edward Thomas, 'Home (3)', *The Collected Poems*, pp. 285–7.
6. Quoted in William Cooke, *Edward Thomas: a Critical Biography, 1878–1917* (London, 1970) p. 38.
7. D. W. Harding, 'A Note on Nostalgia', *Scrutiny*, vol. 1, no. 1, May 1932, pp. 9,17.
8. Ibid., p. 18.
9. Helen Thomas, *As It Was* and *World Without End* (London, 1972) p. 41.
10. Ibid., p. 92.
11. Edward Thomas, 'The long small room', *The Collected Poems*, p. 369.
12. Edward Thomas, *The Childhood*, pp. 13–14.
13. T. S. Eliot, 'To Walter de la Mare', *Collected Poems 1909-1962*, p. 233.
14. Edward Thomas, *The Childhood*, p. 14.
15. Ibid., pp. 39–40.
16. Ibid., p. 17.
17. Ibid., p. 55.
18. Ibid., pp. 90–1.
19. Ibid., pp. 91–2.
20. Ibid., p. 123.
21. Ibid., p. 95.
22. Ibid., pp. 50–1.
23. Ibid., p. 129.
24. Ibid., p. 132.
25. Ibid., p. 134.

26. Ibid., p. 75.
27. Ibid., p. 43.
28. Ibid., pp. 97–8.
29. Ibid., pp. 134–5.
30. Richard Jefferies, *The Gamekeeper at Home* and *The Amateur Poacher* (Oxford University Press, 1978) p. 247.
31. Edward Thomas, *The Diary of Edward Thomas, 1 January – 8 April, 1917, The Collected Poems*, p. 481.
32. Edward Thomas, *The Childhood*, p. 138.
33. Helen Thomas, *As It Was*, p. 34.
34. Edward Thomas, 'Last Poem [The sorrow of true love]', *The Collected Poems*, p. 377.
35. Edward Thomas, 'Rain', *The Collected Poems*, p. 259.
36. Wlliam Empson, 'Just a Smack at Auden', *Collected Poems* (London, 1969) p. 62.
37. Edward Thomas, 'Lights Out', *The Collected Poems*, p. 367.
38. Edward Thomas, *The Diary, The Collected Poems*, p. 481.

CHAPTER 2: TOAD EATING: IVOR GURNEY

1. *The Oxford Book of Twentieth Century English Verse*, pp. 264–5.
2. Two volumes of verse were published in Gurney's life-time: *Severn and Somme*, 1917 and *War's Embers*, 1919.
3. Philip Larkin, Preface to *The Oxford Book of Twentieth Century English Verse*, p. v.
4. F. R. Leavis, 'Auden, Bottrall and Others', *Scrutiny* vol. III, no. 1 (June 1934) p. 72.
5. D. W. Harding, 'The Solid Virtues' (A review of *Claudius The God* by Robert Graves), *Scrutiny*, vol. III, no. 4 (March 1935) p. 422.
6. In *New Bearings in English Poetry* (London 1932; new edition 1950), F. R. Leavis refers to Graves's 'superb autobiography' (p. 58). Unfortunately, but characteristically, the passage adduced relates an anecdote confirming – in Leavis's words – the 'naive conservatism' of Hardy's poems. On the other hand, Leavis's generous discussion of Edward Thomas in the same chapter ('The Situation at the End of World War I') must not be forgotten: 'He was exquisitely sincere and sensitive, and he succeeded in expressing in poetry a representative modern sensibility. It was an achievement of a very rare order, and he has not yet had the recognition he deserves' (p. 72).
7. D. W. Harding; 'Aspects of the Poetry of Isaac Rosenberg', *Scrutiny*, vol. III, no. 4 (March 1935) p. 358.
8. Ibid., p. 363.
9. Walt Whitman, 'As I Lay with my Head in Your Lap Camerado', *The Complete Poems* (Penguin Education, 1975) p. 346.
10. T. S. Eliot, 'Tradition and the Individual Talent', *Selected Essays* (London, 1951) p. 17.
11. D. W. Harding, 'Aspects of the Poetry of Isaac Rosenberg', p. 363.
12. Edmund Blunden, *Undertones of War* (London, 1928; reissued Penguin Books, 1982) pp. 66–7.

13. Wilfred Mellers, 'Ivor Gurney and the English Art-Song', *Scrutiny*, vol. VII, no. 3 (December, 1938) p. 333.
14. Helen Thomas, *Time and Again: memoirs and letters* (Manchester, 1978) pp. 110–12.
15. Edward Thomas, 'When first', *The Collected Poems*, p. 345.
16. Edmund Blunden, 'Concerning Ivor Gurney', *Poems By Ivor Gurney* (London, 1954) p. 10.
17. Ibid., pp. 12–13.
18. Edward Thomas, 'Words', *The Collected Poems*, pp. 217–19.
19. Edward Thomas, 'England', *A language not to be betrayed: Selected prose of Edward Thomas* (Manchester, 1981) pp. 229–30.
20. Edward Thomas, 'Home (1)', *The Collected Poems*, p. 117.
21. Edward Thomas, 'Lights Out', *The Collected Poems*, p. 367.
22. Edward Thomas, 'On Roads and Footpaths', *A language not be be betrayed*, pp. 214–15.
23. Ivor Gurney, 'Roads – Those Roads', *Collected Poems of Ivor Gurney* (Oxford, 1982) p. 140.
24. Edward Thomas, 'Roads', *The Collected Poems*, p. 267.
25. Edward Thomas, *The Diary, The Collected Poems*, p. 466.
26. Ibid., pp. 479–80.
27. Ibid., p. 481.
28. Ivor Gurney, 'Blighty', *Collected Poems*, p. 71.
29. Edmund Blunden, *Undertones of War*, pp. 128–9.
30. Siegfried Sassoon, *The Complete Memoirs of George Sherston: Memoirs of an Infantry Officer* (London, 1937; reprinted London, 1972) pp. 289–90.
31. Frank Richards, *Old Soldiers Never Die* (London, 1933) p. 227.
32. See Tony Ashworth, *Trench Warfare, 1914–1918: The Live and Let Live System* (London, 1980) pp. 21–22 and *passim*.
33. Ibid., pp. 83–4.
34. Frederick Manning, *Her Privates We* (London, 1929; reissued as *The Middle Parts of Fortune*, London, 1977) pp. 216–17. Trevor Wilson, *The Myriad Faces of War: Britain and the Great War, 1914–1918* (Cambridge, 1986) pp. 678–84, writes about this passage: I am indebted to his discussion.
35. Edmund Blunden, *Undertones of War*, p. 231.
36. Siegfried Sassoon, 'Sick Leave', *The War Poems of Siegfried Sassoon* (London, 1983) p. 94.
37. Ivor Gurney, *War Letters* (Manchester, 1983) pp. 127–28. 'Pain', *Collected Poems*, p. 36 is the version quoted here.
38. Rupert Brooke, 'The Dead', *The Collected Poems* (London, 1942) p. 148.
39. Siegfried Sassoon, 'Attack', *The War Poems*, p. 95.
40. Geoffrey Hill, 'Gurney's Hobby', *Essays in Criticism* vol. XXXIV, no. 2 (April 1984) suggests, however, 'the push of the denunciation is toward a crying-out *at* God', p. 116.
41. Leon Wolff, *In Flanders Fields; The 1917 Campaign* (Penguin Books, 1987) pp. 48–9.
42. Ivor Gurney, *War Letters*, pp. 207–8.

43. Ivor Gurney, 'The Escape', *Collected Poems*, p. 117.
44. Ivor Gurney, *War Letters*, p. 74.
45. Ibid., pp. 92–3.
46. Quoted in Eric Leed *No Man's Land: Combat and Identity in World War I* (Cambridge, 1979) p. 126.
47. Ibid.
48. Ibid., p. 131.
49. T. S. Eliot, 'A Note on War Poetry', *Collected Poems 1909–1962*, p. 229.
50. William Carlos Williams, *The Collected Earlier Poems of William Carlos Williams* (London, 1951) p. 241.
51. Ivor Gurney, 'On Somme', *Collected Poems*, p. 157.
52. *O.E.D.* (Second Edition) cites Kipling, *The New Army in Training*, 1915, Ch.11, p. 10 'and the squads at bayonet-practice, had their balance, drive, and recover already.'
53. Ivor Gurney, 'Poem', *Collected Poems*, p. 116.
54. Ivor Gurney, 'Midnight', *Collected Poems*, p. 108.
55. Ivor Gurney, 'Quiet Fireshine', *Collected Poems*, pp. 122–3.
56. Ivor Gurney, 'Friendly Are Meadows', *Collected Poems*, p. 120.
57. William Wordsworth, 'Resolution and Independence', *Poetical Works* (Oxford, 1950) p. 156.
58. Ivor Gurney, *War Letters*, p. 252.
59. P. J. Kavanagh, Introduction to *Collected Poems of Ivor Gurney*, pp. 8–9.
60. Ibid., p. 6.
61. See Anthony Boden, *Stars In A Dark Night, The Letters of Ivor Gurney to the Chapman Family* (London, 1986) p. 107.
62. Ibid.
63. Ivor Gurney, *War Letters*, p. 76.
64. Frank Richards, *Old Soldiers Never Die*, pp. 169–70.
65. Edmund Blunden, *Undertones of War*, pp. 142–3.
66. Robert Graves, *Goodbye to All That* (London, 1929; reissued Penguin Books, 1960) pp. 68–71.
67. Ibid., p. 147.
68. Quoted in Anthony Babington, *For the Sake of Example: Capital Courts Martial 1914–20* (London, 1985) p. 7.
69. Ivor Gurney, *War Letters*, p. 126.
70. Ivor Gurney, 'The Bohemians', *Collected Poems*, p. 174.
71. Quoted in Leon Wolff, *In Flanders Fields*, p. 229. However, one should note that Wolff's reporter is apparently inaccurate about these numbers: according to Babington, eighteen men were shot for cowardice between 1914 and 1920 but no officers. Two officers were shot for desertion and one for murder; *For the Sake of Example* p. 245.
72. W. B. Yeats, 'Vacillation', *The Collected Poems of W. B. Yeats* (London, 1950) p. 283.
73. J. W. Lambert, 'Introduction' to *The Bodley Head Saki* (London, 1963) p. 55.
74. Leon Wolff, *In Flanders Fields*, p. 307.

75. Ivor Gurney, 'The Silent One', *Collected Poems*, p. 102.
76. Geoffrey Hill, 'Gurney's Hobby', p. 112.
77. Ibid., p. 113.
78. Ibid., p. 114.
79. Anthony Babington, *For the Sake of Example*, p. 196.
80. Siegfried Sassoon, 'Memorial Tablet', *The War Poems*, p. 137.
81. Leon Wolff, *In Flanders Fields*, p. 94.
82. Ibid., p. 96.
83. Trevor Wilson, *The Myriad Faces of War*, p. 483 and Wolff, *In Flanders Fields*, pp. 304–7.
84. Philip Warner, *Passchendaele: The Story Behind the Tragic Victory of 1917* (London, 1987) p. 1.
85. Quoted in Trevor Wilson, *The Myriad Faces of War*, p. 473.
86. Quoted in Lyn Macdonald, *They Called it Passchendaele: The Story of the Third Battle of Ypres and the Men Who Fought in It* (London, 1983) pp. 186–7.
87. Ivor Gurney, *War Letters*, p. 193.
88. Ibid., p. 194.
89. Michael Hurd, *The Ordeal of Ivor Gurney* (Oxford, 1984) p. 101.
90. Edwin Campion Vaughan, *Some Desperate Glory: The diary of a young officer, 1917* (London, 1985) p. 199.
91. Dante, *The Inferno of Dante Alighieri*, *The Temple Classics* (London; 1900 reset 1932) pp. 358–9.
92. Edwin Campion Vaughan, *Some Desperate Glory*, pp. 224–5; 228.
93. Ibid., p. 232.
94. Leon Wolff, *In Flanders Fields*, p. 297.
95. Edwin Campion Vaughan, *Some Desperate Glory*, 'About the Diarest', p. xvii.
96. Edmund Blunden, 'Third Ypres', *Undertones of War*, p. 260.
97. Ivor Gurney, 'What's In Time', *Collected Poems*, p. 248.
98. Ivor Gurney, 'O Tan-Faced Prairie Boy', *Collected Poems*, p. 251.
99. Walt Whitman, 'O Tan-Faced Prairie-Boy', *The Complete Poems*, p. 344.
100. Ivor Gurney, 'Chance to Work', *Collected Poems*, p. 268.
101. Michael Hurd, *The Ordeal of Ivor Gurney*, p. 109.
102. Ivor Gurney, *War Letters*, p. 198.
103. Ibid., p. 199.
104. Michael Hurd, *The Ordeal of Ivor Gurney*, p. 104.
105. Ivor Gurney, *War Letters*, p. 201.
106. Paul Fussell, *The Great War and Modern Memory* (Oxford, 1977) pp. 182–6.
107. Ivor Gurney, *War Letters*, p. 230.
108. L. F. Haber, *The Poisonous Cloud; Chemical Warfare in the First World War* (Oxford, Clarendon Press, 1986) p. 192.
109. Ibid., p. 195.
110. Ibid., p. 203.
111. Ibid., pp. 255–56.
112. Ivor Gurney, *War Letters*, p. 198.
113. Ibid.

114. Wilfred Owen, 'Dulce et Decorum Est', *The Collected Poems of Wilfred Owen* (London, 1963) p. 55.
115. See F. L. Haber, *The Poisonous Cloud*, pp. 230–1.
116. Michael Hurd, *The Ordeal of Ivor Gurney*, p. 103.
117. Ivor Gurney, *War Letters*, p. 189.
118. Michael Hurd, *The Ordeal of Ivor Gurney*, p. 104.
119. Ibid.
120. F. L. Haber, *The Poisonous Cloud*, p. 104. Compare Richard Aldington's account of a phosgene attack in *Death Of A Hero* (London, 1929; reissued 1984) pp. 307–15.
121. Ibid., p. 83.
122. Ibid., p. 255.
123. Ibid., p. 256.
124. Ibid., pp. 257–8. But see W. H. Trethowan, 'Ivor Gurney's Mental Illness', *Music and Letters*, vol. 62: 3–4 (July–October 1981), p. 302: 'He remained [at Dartford] until his death from tuberculosis, a common fate of patients with schizophrenia in the days before modern treatment.'
125. Ivor Gurney, 'War Books', *Collected Poems*, p. 196.
126. Eric Leed, *No Man's Land*, p. 4.
127. J. M. Winter, *The Great War and the British People* (London, 1986) p. 291.
128. Ibid., p. 294.
129. C. E. Montague, *Disenchantment* (London, 1922; reprinted 1924) p. 201.
130. Eric J. Leed, *No Man's Land*, p. 187.
131. C. E. Montague, *Disenchantment*, pp. 56–7.
132. See Arthur Marwick, *The Deluge: British Society and the First World War* (London, 1978) p. 283.
133. Trevor Wilson, *The Myriad Faces of War*, p. 769.
134. See Michael Hurd, *The Ordeal of Ivor Gurney*, pp. 127–8.
135. Ibid., pp. 145–6.
136. Ibid., p. 127.
137. Ivor Gurney, 'Sonnet – September 1922', *Collected Poems*, p. 149.
138. Jon Silkin, *Out of Battle; The Poetry of the Great War* (Oxford, 1972) p. 125.
139. Gerard Manley Hopkins, 'The Windhover', *The Poems of Gerard Manley Hopkins* (Oxford, 1967) p. 69.
140. Rudyard Kipling, 'Pagett, M. P.', *Rudyard Kipling's Verse, Inclusive Edition*, 1885–1932 (London, 1933) p. 26.
141. Ivor Gurney, 'Of Cruelty', *Collected Poems*, pp. 195–6.
142. Iona and Peter Opie, *The Lore and Language of School Children* (Oxford, Clarendon Press, 1959) p. 283.
143. Ivor Gurney, 'December 30th', *Collected Poems*, p. 200.
144. Ivor Gurney, 'To God', *Collected Poems*, p. 156.
145. Ivor Gurney, 'The Lock Keeper', *Collected Poems*, pp. 105–6.
146. Ivor Gurney, 'Poem for End', *Collected Poems*, p. 201.
147. Edmund Blunden, 'Concerning Ivor Gurney', *Poems By Ivor Gurney*, p. 19.

148. Ivor Gurney, 'Poem for End', *Collected Poems*, p. 202.
149. Ivor Gurney, 'The Dancers', *Collected Poems*, p. 211.

CHAPTER 3: MY DOG AND MYSELF: J. R. ACKERLEY

1. J. R. Ackerley, *The Letters of J. R. Ackerley* (London, 1975) p. 239. Peter Parker's *Ackerley: The Life of J. R. Ackerley* appeared after this book had gone to press.
2. J. R. Ackerley, *My Father and Myself* (London, 1968; reissued Penguin Books, 1984) pp. 120–2.
3. W. H. Auden, 'Papa Was A Wise Old Sly-Boots' in *Forewords and Afterwords* (London, 1973) p. 458.
4. J. R. Ackerley, *My Father and Myself*, p. 123.
5. Charles Baudelaire, *Mon Coeur Mis à Nu* in *Oeuvres Complètes* (Paris, 1968) p. 624.
6. T. S. Eliot, 'Baudelaire', *Selected Essays*, p. 426.
7. J. R. Ackerley, *My Father and Myself*, p. 89.
8. Ibid., p. 90.
9. Charles Baudelaire, *Mon Coeur Mis à Nu*, p. 632.
10. J. R. Ackerley, *The Letters of J. R. Ackerley*, p. 115.
11. Stephen Spender, 'The Cult of Joe', *The New York Review of Books*, Sept. 16, 1976, p. 26.
12. R. C. Sherriff, *Journey's End* (London, 1929; reissued Penguin Books, 1983) pp. 94–5.
13. Ibid., pp. 62–3.
14. J. R. Ackerley, *The Letters of J. R. Ackerley*, p. 112.
15. J. R. Ackerley, 'Introduction: The Grim Game of Escape' to *Escapers All: The Personal Narratives of Fifteen Escapers from War-Time Prison Camps, 1914–1918* (London, 1932) p. 16.
16. Ibid.
17. Ibid., p. 8.
18. Ibid., p. 16.
19. J. R. Ackerley, *The Prisoners of War* (London, 1925) pp. 32–35.
20. Ibid., p. 36.
21. Ibid., p. 80.
22. J. R. Ackerley, *Escapers All*, p. 16.
23. J. R. Ackerley, *The Prisoners of War*, p. 85.
24. J. R. Ackerley, *My Father and Myself*, p. 43.
25 . Ibid., pp. 44–5.
26. Ibid., p. 46.
27. Ibid., pp. 46–7.
28. Ibid., p. 48.
29. 'Another company commander was Capt. W. P. Nevill of the 8th East Surreys. Nevill was a young officer who liked to stand on the fire-step each evening and shout insults at the Germans. His men were to be in the first wave of the assault near Montauban and he was concerned as to how they would behave, for they had never taken part in an attack before. While he was on leave, Nevill bought four footballs, one for each of his platoons. Back in the trenches, he offered a prize

to the first platoon to kick its football up to the German trenches on
the day of the attack. One platoon painted the following inscription
on its ball:

> The Great European Cup
> The Final
> East Surreys v Bavarians
> Kick Off at Zero'

(Martin Middlebrook, *The First Day on the Somme*, 1 July 1916,
pp. 86–7)

30. Ibid., pp. 49–52
31. Ibid., p. 55.
32. Ibid., pp. 57–8.
33. Ibid., p. 59.
34. Ibid., p. 60.
35. Ibid., pp. 60–1.
36. Ibid., p. 61.
37. Ibid., pp. 61–2.
38. Ibid., p. 64.
39. Ibid., pp. 64–5.
40. Ibid., p. 65.
41. Ibid., p. 136.
42. Ibid., pp. 18–19.
43. Ibid., pp. 20–21.
44. Ibid., p. 22.
45. Ibid., p. 23.
46. Ibid., p. 25.
47. Ibid., p. 29.
48. Ibid., p. 30.
49. Ibid., p. 163.
50. Ibid., p. 162.
51. Ibid., p. 170.
52. Ibid., pp. 118–19.
53. Ibid., p. 171.
54. Ibid., pp. 136–7. For a story of the other family, see Diana Petre,
    The Secret Orchard of Roger Ackerley (London, 1975).
55. Ibid., p. 144.
56. Francis King, Introduction to *Micheldever & Other Poems* by
    J. R. Ackerley (London, 1972) pp. 7–8.
57. J. R. Ackerley, *Hindoo Holiday, An Indian Journal* (London, 1932;
    reissued Penguin Books, 1983) p. 225.
58. J. R. Ackerley, *My Father and Myself*, pp. 78–9.
59. Ibid., pp. 145–6.
60. Ibid., p. 125.
61. Ibid., pp. 128–9.
62. Ibid., p. 129.
63. Ibid., p. 132.
64. Ibid., p. 129.
65. Ibid., pp. 109–110.

66. Ibid., pp. 189–90.
67. J. R. Ackerley, *My Sister and Myself; The Diaries of J. R. Ackerley* (London, 1982).
68. J. R. Ackerley, *My father and Myself*, p. 190.
69 . Francis King, *Introduction to Micheldever & Other Poems* p. 9.
70. J. R. Ackerley, *Hindoo Holiday*, p. 247.
71. Ibid., pp. 217–18.
72. J. R. Ackerley, *My Father and Myself*, pp. 190–1.
73. Ibid., p. 191.
74. J. R. Ackerley, *My Dog Tulip* (London, 1956) pp. 138–9.
75. *My Dog Tulip* (New York, 1965) p. 157.
76. J. R. Ackerley, *My Sister and Myself*, p. 197.
77. Ibid., p. 206.
78. J. R. Ackerley, *My Father and Myself*, p. 192.
79. J. R. Ackerley, *The Letters of J. R. Ackerley*, p. 241.
80. J. R. Ackerley, *My Dog Tulip* (London ed.) p. 153–4.
81. Ibid., p. 154–5.
82. J. R. Ackerley, *My Father and Myself*, p. 190.
83. Francis King, Introduction to J. R. Ackerley, *My Sister and Myself*, p. 11.
84. J. R. Ackerley, *We Think the World of You* (London, 1960) p. 78.
85. Ibid., p. 116.
86. Ibid., p. 155.
87. Ibid., pp. 157–8.
88. Stuart Hampshire, 'Truth in Fiction' (A Review of *We Think the World of You*) *Encounter* (London) vol. 16, no. 5 (1961) p. 80.
89. Ibid., p. 81.
90. Ibid., p. 79.
91. J. R. Ackerley, *Hindoo Holiday*, pp. 259–60.
92. J. R. Ackerley, 'After the blitz, 1941', *Micheldever & Other Poems*, p. 27.

Select Bibliography

PRIMARY AUTHORS

ACKERLEY, J. R., *Poems by Four Authors* (Cambridge, 1923) includes ten poems by Ackerley.

ACKERLEY, J. R., *The Prisoners of War* (London, 1925).

ACKERLEY, J. R., *Hindoo Holiday: An Indian Journal* (London 1932, reissued Penguin Books, 1983).

ACKERLEY, J. R., *Escapers All: The Personal Narratives of Fifteen Escapers from War-Time Prison Camps, 1914–1918*, edited with an Introduction by Ackerley, London, 1932.

ACKERLEY, J. R., *My Dog Tulip* (London, 1956; revised 1966).

ACKERLEY, J. R., *We Think the World of You: A Novel* (London, 1960).

ACKERLEY, J. R., *My Dog Tulip* (New York, 1965).

ACKERLEY, J. R., *My Father and Myself: A Family Memoir* (London, 1968; reissued Penguin Books, 1984).

ACKERLEY, J. R., *E. M. Forster: A Portrait* (London, 1970).

ACKERLEY, J. R., *Micheldever & Other Poems*, edited with an Introduction by Francis King (London, 1972).

ACKERLEY, J. R., *The Letters of J. R. Ackerley*, edited by Neville Braybrooke (London, 1975).

ACKERLEY, J. R., *My Sister and Myself: The Diaries of J. R. Ackerley*, edited with an Introduction by Francis King (London, 1982).

ACKERLEY, J. R., 'My Dog Tulip', *Encounter* vol. II, no. 3 (London, 1954) pp. 7–15.

ACKERLEY, J. R., 'A Summer's Evening', *London Magazine* vol. 9, no. 7 (October 1969) pp. 39–46.

BAUDELAIRE, C., *Oeuvres Complètes*, Préface, Présentation et Notes de M. A. Ruff (Paris, 1968).

BLUNDEN, E., *Undertones of War*, with a Supplement of Poetical Interpretations and Variations (London, 1928; reissued Penguin Books, 1982).

BLUNDEN, E., 'A Booklist on the War, 1914–1918' compiled by Edmund Blunden, Captain Cyril Falls, H. M. Tomlinson and Captain R. Wright with an Introduction by Edmund Blunden (London, 1930).

BLUNDEN, E., 'Concerning Ivor Gurney' in *Poems By Ivor Gurney* (London, 1954).

BROOKE, R., *The Collected Poems*, with a Memoir by Edward Marsh (London, 1918; 3rd revised edition, 1942).

DANTE, *The Inferno of Dante Alighieri*, Temple Classics (London, 1900, reset 1932).

ELIOT, T. S., *Collected Poems 1909–1962* (London, 1963; 3rd impression, 1966).

ELIOT, T. S., *Selected Essays* (London, 1932; 3rd enlarged edition, 1951).

ELIOT, T. S., *On Poetry and Poets* (London, 1957).

ELIOT, T. S., *The Letters of T. S. Eliot Volume 1 1898–1922*, edited by Valerie Eliot (London, 1988).

FARJEON, E., *Edward Thomas: The Last Four Years* (Oxford, 1958; reissued 1979).

FORSTER, E. M., *A Passage to India* (London, 1924).

FORSTER, E. M., *The Hill of Devi* (London, 1953).

GRAVES, R., *Goodbye to All That* (London, 1929; revised 1957, reissued Penguin Books, 1960).

GURNEY, I., *Severn and Somme* (London, 1917; reprinted 1919).

GURNEY, I., *War's Embers* (London, 1919).

GURNEY, I., "A Symposium" (apart from the music, includes an essay by Marion Scott and brief essays on the poems by J. C. Squire, Walter de la Mare and Edmund Blunden) *Music and Letters*, vol. XIX, no. 1 (Jan. 1938) pp. 1–17.

GURNEY, I., *Poems By Ivor Gurney*, principally selected from unpublished manuscripts with a Memoir by Edmund Blunden (London, 1954).

GURNEY, I., *Poems of Ivor Gurney, 1890–1937*, chosen by Leonard Clark with an Introduction by Edmund Blunden and a Biographical Note by Leonard Clark (London, 1973).

GURNEY, I., *Collected Poems of Ivor Gurney*, chosen, edited with an Introduction by P. J. Kavanagh (Oxford, 1982).

GURNEY, I., *Ivor Gurney, War Letters*, a selection edited by R. K. R. Thornton (Manchester, 1983).

GURNEY, I., *Stars In A Dark Night, the Letters of Ivor Gurney to the Chapman Family*, edited by Anthony Boden with a Foreword by Michael Hurd (Gloucester, 1986).

HARDY, T., *The Complete Poems of Thomas Hardy*, edited by James Gibson (London, 1976).

HURD, M. *The Ordeal of Ivor Gurney* (Oxford, 1978; reissued 1984).

LARKIN, P., *The Oxford Book of Twentieth Century English Verse*, chosen by Philip Larkin (Oxford, 1973; reprinted with corrections, 1974).

LARKIN, P., *Required Writing: Miscellaneous Pieces 1955–1982* (London, 1983).

LARKIN, P., *Collected Poems*, edited with an Introduction by Anthony Thwaite (London, 1988).

MACDONALD, L., *They Called It Passchendaele: The Story of the Third Battle of Ypres and the Men Who Fought in It* (London, 1983).

MANNING, F., *Her Privates We* (London, 1929); reissued as *The Middle Parts of Fortune, Somme and Ancre, 1916*, with an Introduction by Michael Howard (London, 1977).

MONTAGUE, C. E., *Disenchantment* (London, 1922; reprinted 1924).

MONTALE, E., *It Depends: A Poet's Notebook* (*Quaderno di quattro anni*), translated and introduced by G. Singh (New York, 1980).

OWEN, W., *The Collected Poems of Wilfred Owen*, edited with an Introduction and Notes by C. Day Lewis (London, 1974).

PETRE, D., *The Secret Orchard of Roger Ackerley* (London, 1975).

RICHARDS, F., *Old Soldiers Never Die* (London, 1933).

SASSOON, S., *The Complete Memoirs of George Sherston* (London 1937; reissued 1972).

SASSOON, S., *Siegfried's Journey 1916–20* (London, 1945; reissued 1982).

SASSOON, S., *Siegfried Sassoon Diaries 1920–1922*, edited and introduced by Rupert Hart-Davis (London, 1981).

SASSOON, S., *The War Poems of Siegfried Sassoon*, arranged and introduced by Rupert Hart-Davis (London, 1983).

SHERRIFF, R. C., *Journey's End* (London, 1929; reissued Penguin Books, 1983).

SIMMEL, G., *On Individuality and Social Forms, Selected Writings*, edited with an Introduction by Donald N. Levine (Chicago, 1971).

THOMAS, E., *The Childhood of Edward Thomas, a fragment of autobiography*, (London, 1938; reissued with a Preface by Roland Gant, 1983).

THOMAS, E., *The Collected Poems of Edward Thomas*, edited and introduced by R. George Thomas (Oxford, 1978).

THOMAS, E., *Edward Thomas: Selected Poems and Prose*, edited with an Introduction by David Wright (Harmondsworth, 1981).

THOMAS, E., *A Language Not to be Betrayed: Selected prose of Edward Thomas*, selected with an Introduction by Edna Longley (Manchester, 1981).

THOMAS, E., *Edward Thomas's Letters to Jesse Berridge*, with a Memoir by Jesse Berridge, edited and introduced by Anthony Berridge (London, 1983).

THOMAS, H., *As It Was* and *World Without End* (London, 1935; reissued 1972).

THOMAS, H., *Time and Again, memoirs and letters*, edited by Myfanwy Thomas (Manchester, 1978).

THOMAS, M., *One of These Fine Days: Memoirs* (Manchester, 1982).

VAUGHAN, E. C., *Some Desperate Glory: The diary of a young officer, 1917* (London, 1985).

WHITMAN, W., *The Complete Poems*, edited by Francis Murphy (Harmondsworth 1975).

OTHER WORKS

ALDINGTON, R., *Death of a Hero* (London, 1929; reissued with a new Introduction by Christopher Ridgway, London, 1984).

ASHWORTH, T., *Trench Warfare, 1914–1918: The Live and Let Live System* (London, 1980).

AUDEN, W. H., *Forewords and Afterwords* (London, 1973).

BABINGTON, A., *For the Sake of Example: Capital Courts Martial 1914–1920* (London, 1985).

COOKE, W., *Edward Thomas, a Critical Biography, 1878–1917* (London, 1970).

COOMBES, H., *Edward Thomas:A Critical Study* (London, 1956).

DAVIE, D., *Thomas Hardy and British Poetry* (London, 1979).

EMPSON, W., *Collected Poems* (London, 1969).

EVERETT, B., *Poets in Their Time, Essays on English Poets from Donne to Larkin* (London, 1986).

FROST, R., *Selected Letters*, edited by Lawrance Thompson (New York, 1964).

FUSSELL, P., *The Great War and Modern Memory* (Oxford, 1977).

GARDNER, H., *The New oxford Book of English Verse, 1250–1950*, chosen and edited by Helen Gardner (Oxford, 1972).

GITTINGS, R., *The Older Hardy* (Harmondsworth, 1980).

GRAY, T., *The Poems of Gray and Collins*, edited by Austin Lane Poole (Oxford, 1937).

HABER, L. F., *The Poisonous Cloud: Chemical Warfare in the First World War* (Oxford, 1986).

HAMPSHIRE, S., 'Truth in Fiction' (A Review of *We Think the World of You*) *Encounter* vol. 16, no. 5 (London, 1961) pp. 79–81.

HARDING, D. W., 'A Note on Nostalgia', *Scrutiny*, vol. I, no. 1 (May 1932; reprinted Cambridge, 1963) pp. 8–19.

HARDING, D. W., 'The Solid Virtues' (A Review of *Claudius the God* by Robert Graves), *Scrutiny*, vol. III, no. 4 (March 1935; reprinted Cambridge, 1963) pp. 421–2.

HARDING, D. W., 'Aspects of the Poetry of Isaac Rosenberg', *Scrutiny*, vol. III, no. 4 (March 1935; reprinted Cambridge, 1963) pp. 358–69.

HARMAN, L. D., *The Modern Stranger, On Language and Membership* (Berlin, New York, Amsterdam, 1988).

HILL, G., 'Gurney's Hobby', *Essays in Criticism*, vol. XXXIV, no. 2 (April 1984) pp. 97–128.

HOBSBAWM, E., *The Invention of Tradition*, edited by Eric Hobsbawm and Terence Ranger (Cambridge, 1983).

HOPKINS, G. M., *The Poems of Gerard Manley Hopkins* (Fourth Edition) edited by W. H. Gardner and N. H. Mackenzie (Oxford, 1967).

JEFFERIES, R., *The Gamekeeper at Home* (1878) and *The Amateur Poacher* (1879), with an Introduction by Richard Fitter (Oxford, 1978).

KENNER, H., *A Sinking Island: The Modern English Writers* (London, 1987).

KIPLING, R., *The New Army in Training* (London, 1915).

KIPLING, R., *Rudyard Kipling's Verse: Inclusive Edition, 1885–1932* (London, 1933).

LA ROCHEFOUCAULD, *Maximes et Autres Oeuvres Morales* Préface de Jacques de Lacretelle, annotée par Alexandre Borrot (Paris, 1949).

LEAVIS, F. R., *New Bearings in English Poetry* (London, 1932; new edition, 1950).

LEAVIS, F. R., 'Auden, Boltrall and Others', *Scrutiny*, vol. III, no. 1 (June, 1934, reprinted Cambridge, 1963) pp. 70–83.

LEAVIS, F. R., *The Great Tradition* (London, 1948; reissued Peregrine Books, 1962).

'Xenia', in Eugenio Montale, *New Poems, a selection from Satura and Diario del '71 e del '72*, translated and introduced by G. Singh (New York, 1976).

LEED, E., *No Man's Land: Combat and Identity in World War I* (Cambridge, 1979).

LONGLEY, E., *Poetry in the Wars* (Newcastle Upon Tyne, 1986).

MACDONALD, L., *Somme* (London, 1983).

MACDONALD, L., *They Called it Passchendale: The Story of the Third Battle of Ypres and the Men Who Fought in It* (London, 1983).

MARWICK, A., *The Deluge: British Society and the First World War* (London, 1973).

MELLERS, W., 'Ivor Gurney and the English Art-Song', *Scrutiny*, vol. VII, no. 3 (December 1938; reprinted Cambridge, 1963) pp. 332–6.

MIDDLEBROOK, M., *The First Day on the Somme, 1 July 1916* (Harmondsworth 1984).

MILLGATE, M., *Thomas Hardy, a Biography* (Oxford, reprinted with corrections, 1987).

OPIE, I. and P., *The Lore and Language of School Children* (Oxford, 1959).

POE, E. A., *Tales of Mystery and Imagination* (London, 1908).

SAKI, *The Bodley Head Saki*, selected and introduced by J. W. Lambert (London, 1963).

SANTAYANA, G., *Soliloquies in England*, (1914–1918) *And Later Soliloquies*, (1918–1921), (London, 1922).

SHAKESPEARE, W., *Shakespeare's Sonnets*, edited with analytic commentary by Stephen Booth (New Haven and London, 1977).

SILKIN, J., *Out of Battle*; The Poetry of the Great War (Oxford, 1972).

SILKIN, J., *The Penguin Book of First World War Poetry*, edited with an Introduction by Jon Silkin (1979).

SIMPSON, J. A., *The Oxford English Dictionary, Second Edition*, prepared by J. A. Simpson and E. S. C. Weiner (Oxford, 1989).

SPENDER, S., 'The Cult of Joe', *The New York Review of Books*, September 16, 1976, pp. 26–8; 37–8.

TAYLOR, A. J. P., *The First World War: An Illustrated History* (Harmondsworth, 1966).

THOMAS, R. G., *Edward Thomas: A Portrait* (Oxford, 1985).

TRETHOWAN, W. H. , 'Ivor Gurney's Mental Illness', *Music and Letters* vol. 62: 3–4 (July–October 1981) pp. 300–309.

TRILLING, L., *Sincerity and Authenticity* (Oxford, 1972).

TOMLINSON C., 'Ivor Gurney's "Best Poems"', *Times Literary Supplement* January 3, 1986, p. 12.

WALVIN, J., *A Child's World: A Social History of English Childhood, 1800–1914* (Harmondsworth, 1982).

WARNER, P., *Passchendaele: The Story behind the Tragic Victory of 1917* (London, 1987).

WATERMAN, A, 'The Poetic Achievement of Ivor Gurney', *Critical Quarterly* vol. 25 no. 4 (Winter 1983), pp. 3–19

WILLIAMS, R., *The Country and the City* (London, 1973).

WILLIAMS, R., *Politics and Letters, Interviews with New Left Review* (London, 1979).

WILLIAMS, W. C., *The Collected Earlier Poems of William Carlos Williams* (London, 1951).

WILSON, T., *The Myriad Faces of War: Britain and the Great War, 1914–1918* (Cambridge, 1986).

WINTER, J. M., *The Great War and the British People* (London, 1986).

WOLFF L., *In Flanders Fields; The 1917 Campaign* (Harmondsworth, 1979).

WORDSWORTH, W., *Poetical Works*, edited by Thomas Hutchinson, new edition revised by Ernest de Selincourt (Oxford, 1950).

YEATS, W. B., *The Oxford Book of Modern Verse 1892–1935*, chosen by W. B. Yeats (Oxford, 1936).

YEATS, W. B., *The Collected Poems of W.B. Yeats* (London, 1950).

Index